D0361384

APR 16 2019

NO LONGER PROPERTY OF
SEATTLE PUBLIC LIBRARY

WALKING ----→
PORTLAND

 **WILDERNESS PRESS** . . . *on the trail since 1967*

Walking Portland: 33 tours of Stumptown's Funky Neighborhoods, Historic Landmarks, Parks, Farmers Markets, and Brewpubs

Second edition, first printing

Copyright © 2019 and 2013 by Becky Ohlsen

Project editor: Kate Johnson
Maps: Scott McGrew and Tommy Hertzel
Cover and interior design: Jonathan Norberg
Interior photos by Becky Ohlsen except: page 15: ARTYOORAN/Shutterstock.com, page 176: Mike Russell
Copy editor: Susan Roberts McWilliams
Proofreader: Rebecca Henderson
Indexer: Meghan Brawley/Potomac Indexing

Library of Congress Cataloging-in-Publication Data

Names: Ohlsen, Becky, author.
Title: Walking Portland : 33 tours of Stumptown's funky neighborhoods, historic landmarks, parks, farmers
    markets, and brewpubs / Becky Ohlsen.
Other titles: Thirty-three tours of Stumptown's funky neighborhoods, historic landmarks, parks, farmers
    markets, and brewpubs
Description: Second Edition. | Birmingham, Alabama : Wilderness Press, [2019] | "Distributed by Publishers
    Group West"—T.p. verso.
Identifiers: LCCN 2018049779| ISBN 9780899978925 (paperback) | ISBN 9780899978932 (ebook)
Subjects: LCSH: Walking—Oregon—Portland—Guidebooks. | Walking—Oregon—Portland—Tours. |
    Walking—Oregon—Portland Metropolitan Area—Guidebooks. | Portland (Or.)—Guidebooks. |
    Portland Metropolitan Area (Or.)—Guidebooks.
Classification: LCC GV199.42.O72 P676 2019 | DDC 917.95/4904—dc23
LC record available at https://lccn.loc.gov/2018049779

Published by 🐸 **WILDERNESS PRESS**
    An imprint of AdventureKEEN
    2204 First Ave. S., Ste. 102
    Birmingham, AL 35233
    800-443-7227, fax 205-326-1012

Visit wildernesspress.com for a complete listing of our books and for ordering information. Contact us at our website, at facebook.com/wildernesspress1967, or at twitter.com/wilderness1967 with questions or comments. To find out more about who we are and what we're doing, visit blog.wildernesspress.com.

Manufactured in the United States of America

Distributed by Publishers Group West

Frontispiece: A house in Portland's Irvington neighborhood (see Walk 18, page 94)

Cover photo: Oregon Maritime Museum in Tom McCall Waterfront Park (see Walk 10, page 49), Willamette River, Portland, Oregon, USA. Photographed by Ian Dagnall/Alamy Stock Photo

All rights reserved. No part of this book may be reproduced in any form, or by any means electronic, mechanical, recording, or otherwise, without written permission from the publisher, except for brief quotations used in reviews.

SAFETY NOTICE: Although Wilderness Press and the author have made every attempt to ensure that the information in this book is accurate at press time, they are not responsible for any loss, damage, injury, or inconvenience that may occur to anyone while using this book. You are responsible for your own safety and health while following the walking trips described here. Always check local conditions, know your limitations, and consult a map.

WALKING – – – –→
PORTLAND

33 Tours of Stumptown's Funky Neighborhoods, Historic Landmarks, Parks, Farmers Markets, and Brewpubs

Second Edition

Becky Ohlsen

WILDERNESS PRESS . . . *on the trail since 1967*

Acknowledgments

First off, thanks to Molly Merkle, Kate Johnson, and Tim Jackson at Wilderness Press for their patience and help in getting this second edition updated and out the door. Also to fellow walking-guide author and erstwhile Portlander Ryan Ver Berkmoes, who roped me into this project in its early stages and made me realize how much I liked the idea of exploring my own city for a change. I had a lot of help along the way, too, including from Zac Christensen, who hooked me up with Metro trails coordinator Mel Huie; and from Patrick Leyshock, Kate McLaughlin, Zach and Ashton Hull, Mike Russell, DK Holm, Audrey van Buskirk, Susan Wickstrom, Paul Smith, Darrell Fuhriman, and Margo DeBeir, all of whom provided moral support, intel, and even dinner. Finally, thanks to Portland for being such a fun place to write about, and to everyone who's been curious enough about the city to pick up this book as an admittedly biased but hopefully useful guide.

Author's Note

Portland's a great town for walking, especially if you aren't the type who melts in rain. The city is mostly flat, the blocks are much shorter than the usual length (which is really only a help for the ego, but still), and there are gorgeous parks and green spaces blanketing every section of the city. (And it's true what they say about April showers—the flowers here in spring are unbelievable.) If you really aren't the Gene Kelly type, you'll find warm and cozy brewpubs, dive bars, coffee shops, and tea houses to duck into on nearly every block; I've recommended several personal favorites in most of these walks.

Some of the routes here are slightly hilly, and some include unpaved trails through the city's urban forest, so do be prepared and choose your footwear wisely. (Also, unless you're here in August, bring an umbrella or a rain jacket. You'll probably hear people saying that real Portlanders refuse to use umbrellas, but that's a myth.) But Portland has yet another advantage as a walker's paradise: its public transportation system is excellent, so if you wear yourself out, it's usually easy to catch a bus back toward the center of town from most anywhere.

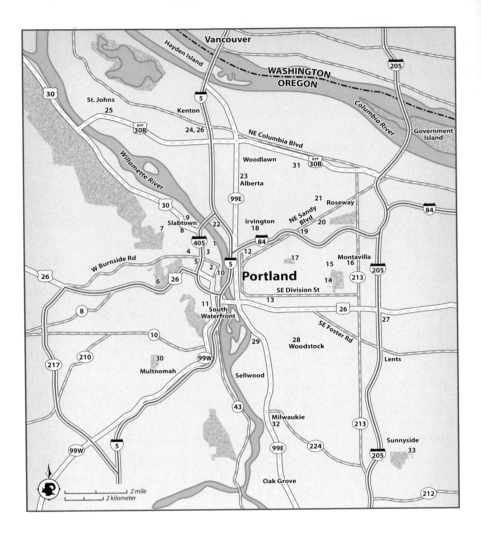

Table of Contents

Introduction

Walking is a great way to think. All the great thinkers have written about it, from Emerson and Thoreau to Nietzsche to Kierkegaard—who is often quoted as having said, "If one just keeps on walking, everything will be alright." (Seems worth a try.) Walking and writing go well together, too—look at Wordsworth, or for something a little more contemporary, Rebecca Solnit, who wrote the wonderful *Wanderlust: A History of Walking* (2012). It sure beats sitting at your desk and struggling to think up something useful to say. Writing, even travel writing, involves an unpleasant amount of sitting at a desk. All morning I dream up excuses, little errands that surely need doing: groceries to pick up, packages to mail, something on hold (or more likely, overdue) at the library.

So if there's one thing I fervently hope for this book, it's that it provides you with a couple dozen good excuses to go outside and take a walk.

In a way, I inherited *Walking Portland*. When I first signed on, the plan was for me to cowrite it with my friend and fellow travel writer Ryan Ver Berkmoes (author of *Walking Chicago*), whom I knew from years of writing for Lonely Planet. He had recently moved to Portland, and we thought it would be fun to team up on a project. Sadly, Ryan's travel schedule kept him on the road approximately 387 days a year, so he had to bow out of *Walking Portland* in the planning stages. But by then I was sold on the idea: here was a chance to explore my own backyard, to write about a place I knew and liked in a more relaxed format than I usually get to do. The book would give me plenty of room for going off on weird tangents, airing petty grievances, and talking up places like the Sandy Hut, a bar I love but that I admit would be a pretty tough sell to, say, a midrange international traveler.

(I guess this is as good a place as any to tell you that the book you are holding may contain tangents, grievances, and recommendations for places that some people might not love. You've been warned.)

Although it works just fine as a travel guide, this book is less about getting from place to place than it is about slowing down and seeing the city in a new way. Portland is growing and changing at breakneck speed. It's hard to keep up, even for someone like me, who's basically paid to keep up. Things move fast: apartments spring up on the tombs of old dive bars; restaurants open to great fanfare, then close again before I have a chance to eat there; entire streets are rerouted or redesigned. The pace of growth in formerly sleepy old

The Saturday Market runs on both Saturdays and Sundays from March until December 24 (see Walk 10: Hawthorne Bridge to Steel Bridge (page 49).

Stumptown is certainly exciting, but also, for some of us, a little alarming. I find that walking is a nice way to slow it all down.

Most of the walks in this book are built for sauntering unambitiously through urban areas with a high potential for distraction and discovery. (A few are more remote, incorporating wide-open meadows, riverside paths, or leafy trails through the woods.) They're easy to customize: you can mix several walks together, do half one day and half the next, get tired and hop a bus, or even just walk vicariously while sitting in a pub, reading the book. I support that approach.

As I noted in the first edition—and it's still true—some of the best things in *Walking Portland* are gone: The steakhouse with deep red booths. The creek that disappears. The pawn shop that used to be a rock club. The building shaped like a shoe. Some of these walks are ghost walks now—so much of what they pass is lost. But there's still a lot in Portland waiting to be found.

In terms of geography, Portland is ideal for walking: it has a compact, almost European-style layout, with an abundance of parks and open spaces—the result of the city's unconventional approach to planning and transportation, especially in its formative early years. Despite its recent rapid growth, Portland still has plenty of odd little nooks and crannies where locals (and visitors in the know) can find room to hang out, relax, and explore ideas like "What if we used bicycles to transport our brewpub around the city," or "How about we put a hotel in that crumbling warehouse?"

A walk in Portland thus is likely to include an element of surprise. On any given stroll, you might round a corner to find a pop-up shop selling vintage paperbacks or gluten-free cupcakes shaped like the mayor (these are made-up examples, but it wouldn't surprise me in the least), and beyond that a manicured Victorian house restored with heart-breaking care. And it may turn out that the beautiful Victorian house is also a coffee shop or a brewpub or both, and so you settle in with your book or cupcake for a pause in its rhododendron-filled back garden.

Granted, for three-fourths of the year this scenario might have a backdrop of rain. Portland is known for its soggy weather, though it's reliably fair and warm (well, some-times ungodly hot and humid) in July and August. And all that rain produces some of the most glorious gardens and parks in the country—even ordinary houses in many neighborhoods boast front yards that are landscaping wonders. If you're a fan of rhodo-dendrons and other flowering trees, don't miss a chance to visit in May or June for epic displays all over town.

The walks we've laid out are neighborhood-focused, so you'll get the flavor of quite a few different parts of the city. This edition includes three new walks and one bonus walk, as well as all new photos and thoroughly updated descriptions of the original 30 routes.

One more thing: I hope readers don't feel completely tied to the routes described here. Veer from the path! Ideally this book should lead you into a neighborhood and give you a general sense of its character, then turn you loose. After all, it's much more fun to discover interesting things on your own. I strongly encourage you to roam as far off the map as you have time for, and let me know what you find. (Please send any comments, complaints, or amazing discoveries you'd like to share with the author to bohlsen@gmail.com or in care of Wilderness Press; our mailing address is on page iv.)

1 Old Town and Chinatown
Skid Row No More

Above: The recently expanded Ground Kontrol arcade

BOUNDARIES: NW Broadway, Willamette River, W. Burnside St.
DISTANCE: 2 miles
DIFFICULTY: Easy
PARKING: Metered street parking
PUBLIC TRANSIT: MAX Green and Yellow Lines (Union Station), Red and Blue Lines
(Old Town/Chinatown Station)

This is the historic core of Portland, once upon a time a rough-and-tumble waterfront where sailors and loggers went carousing in the muddy streets. (Some claim it's the source of the term *Skid Row,* although Seattle also claims that dubious honor. Regardless, the expression refers to the path along which cut logs were ushered toward the river to be shipped.) In those days, before the harbor wall was built to help contain the waters of the Willamette River, this area flooded regularly several times a season. (This was also before an efficient sewer system had been implemented, so you can imagine.) Beneath the streets of Old Town are the legendary Shanghai tunnels, where—rumor has it, though historians dispute it—drunken sailors would be dropped into underground corridors below certain downtown bars, then dragged through the tunnels onto ships, where they would awaken to find themselves indentured workers. You can still tour the Shanghai tunnels below town today.

Like many urban cores, Old Town suffered from a few decades of neglect and was considered a pretty sketchy area until a decade or so ago, when the city's focused attention helped revitalize the neighborhood. That's not to say there are no longer any gritty elements, but these days, Old Town and Chinatown tend to be lively rather than deserted at night, with entertainment options including several good bars and clubs, art galleries, top-notch restaurants, and the Lan Su Chinese Garden, a major draw for visitors.

Part of Old Town's appeal is its historic architecture, particularly its character-rich brick and cast-iron buildings. In fact, Portland has one of the biggest collections of historic cast-iron architecture in the country. Preservation efforts have helped to keep a lot of the city's historical charm intact.

Walk Description

Start at Union Station; its huge clock tower and glowing GO BY TRAIN sign make it a great landmark. It was completed in 1896, not quite as commissioned by writer–turned–railway owner Henry Villard, who went bust before his plans for the station could be completed. A somewhat more modest version of Villard's idea was eventually built, and the interior was later remodeled by Pietro Belluschi, the Italian-born, Portland-based architect behind the famous Pan Am building in New York and whose fingerprints are on buildings all over Oregon (including the Portland Art Museum, several churches, and buildings at Reed College and Willamette University). The station is now owned and maintained by the Portland Development Commission. Attached to the station is a fittingly old-school restaurant/piano bar, Wilf's, with red-velvet wingback chairs, brick walls, chandeliers, and live jazz most nights.

From Union Station, walk south along Northwest Sixth Avenue. Turn left at Northwest Everett, and walk three blocks. At Northwest Third and Everett is ❶ Lan Su Chinese Garden. The idea of the garden was initially sparked when Portland established a sister-city relationship with Suzhou, China; gradually, momentum grew, funds were raised, and plans were made. The garden opened in September 2000, adding an important degree of solidity to the hopeful notion that Old Town was really on its way up. A big draw for visitors as well as an oasis for downtown office workers, the garden is a tranquil and restorative place (especially remarkable considering its location), and it has

Backstory: Pinball in Peril

These days, Portland is one of the pinball capitals of the United States, with nearly 800 machines in more than 300 venues. By some counts, we have more pinball games per capita than New York or Los Angeles. Nearly every dive bar worth its salt has at least a machine or two, and some of the best bars in town make it a point to be sought out specifically as pinball destinations, keeping popular machines in circulation and tuned up to perfection. The great 'zine *Multiball*, which at its peak in the late 1990s and early 2000s was distributing 4,000 copies across the United States, was produced in Portland. There are at least two, arguably three, dedicated pinball halls in town. Scrappy pinball clubs battle it out on a regular basis in tournaments. In short, it's a thriving scene. But once upon a time, pinball (in Portland as in many other cities) was seen as a terrible vice, falling into the same category as prostitution, gambling, and unlicensed alcohol sales. (People back then used to bet on pinball scores, and some of the machines actually paid out—imagine! It sounds almost too good to be true, until you realize that many of the machines back then didn't have flippers, so they really were games of chance, not skill.) In the 1950s a shady guy called Jim Elkins ran the pinball racket in Portland, with cooperation from a well-greased police force, until he got too big for his britches and, after some ill-thought-out provocation, was run out of the game by a rival who had the backing of the Teamsters. It wasn't until many years later that city officials recognized what all of us who play pinball know to be true: although it's a ton of fun, pinball is even less likely to be profitable than slot machines or video poker. *Sigh.*

that magical ability to seem much larger on the inside than it looks from the outside. There's also an adjoining tea shop where you can sample a wide range of traditional teas and light snacks.

From Everett, turn right onto Northwest Second Avenue, then right again on Northwest Davis. At Northwest Sixth Avenue turn left; halfway down this block, on your right (at 125 NW Sixth Ave.), was once Satyricon, the longest-running punk club on the West Coast, something like the Portland equivalent of CBGB (and similarly nonexistent today). It's hard to overestimate the importance of the club to Portland's live-music scene and equally tough to imagine a venue today where you could see so many awesome bands in such a small space—Nirvana opened for Mudhoney here in 1989, to give just one example. The capacity was about 200 people.

Satyricon closed for good in 2010 (after having closed temporarily in 2003, turned into a soulless club called Icon, closed briefly again, then revived as an all-ages nightclub), and the building was torn down, an event that, apart from being very sad, must have smelled terrible. (Satyricon's men's room, for years, featured a communal trough—enough said?)

On Northwest Couch Street, turn left, and you'll reach ❷ **Ground Kontrol,** a playground for Portland-style grown-ups, aka permanent adolescents. It has all the arcade games you either remember from your youth or wish you'd had when you were a kid. (A recent expansion means there are even more games available these days—the place is now about twice its original size.) The pinball collection alone is awesome. And they're all still cheap to play. After 5 p.m., there is also beer for the over-21 crowd, and the space occasionally serves as a live-music venue.

At Northwest Fifth Avenue turn right, then turn left on West Burnside Street for a block. At Burnside and Northwest Fourth Avenue is the 38-foot-tall Chinatown Gate, installed in 1986; turn left on Fourth to pass through it. The gate is just about the only remnant left of what used

Union Station

to be considered Portland's Chinatown. Most of the shops and restaurants that were once here have moved to outer southeast Portland, along with much of the city's Chinese population, to what's known as the Jade District. That's not to say there's nothing going on here; this district has been perking up lately.

At Northwest Fourth Avenue and Couch Street is a good comic-book shop, ❸ **Floating World Comics.** (In Portland, if it's not clear by now, comics are indisputably cool, not nerdy— although are comics really still considered nerdy anywhere? What used to be called geek culture has long since gone mainstream.) Kitty-corner from Floating World is a beloved relic from a few years back, the enormous neon sign for the long-departed Chinese restaurant Hung Far Low. (It's OK if you can't keep a straight face.) Dedicated barflies adored Hung Far Low for the minuscule corner bar, dark as night, with its tiny, cheap, and powerful drinks; impassive bartenders; glowing Buddha statue; and perilously long, narrow staircase that led up from the street. When it closed (and moved to Southeast 82nd Avenue, along with many of the other businesses that once inhabited historic Chinatown—only to close again in 2015, this time for good), a touchingly sincere effort was made to preserve and keep displaying the Hung Far Low sign. It worked.

Having turned right on Couch, turn right again on Northwest Third Avenue, then left on West Burnside, left again on Northwest Second Avenue, and then right to get back to Northwest Couch. These blocks contain some of the grittier street life in the area, as well as some of the more memorable old buildings.

Follow Couch to Northwest Naito Parkway and turn right. From here you have an interesting view of the White Stag sign, a beloved local landmark and yet another beneficiary of the Old Town preservationist spirit. (It's been changed several times to suit whichever business was using it to advertise, but the sign's original makers donated it to the city in 2010.)

Walk underneath the Burnside Bridge—a part of town that exists in sharp contrast to the gleaming new developments at either end of the bridge—and turn right at Southwest Ankeny Street, where you'll see the Skidmore Fountain and Ira Kel. The fountain is from 1888 and was intended for "horses, men, and dogs," but drink at your own risk. This area is part of the grounds of Portland's Saturday Market, which we'll cover in Walk 10: Hawthorne Bridge to Steel Bridge (page 49).

Continue straight on Southwest Ankeny Street, and you'll come to an alleyway shared by several bars in the block. Here again, drink at your own risk—but this is a fun and lively hangout, especially in warm weather, and the surrounding bars are all worth investigating if it's too cold for sitting outdoors. Be sure to step into ❹ **Dan & Louis Oyster Bar,** one of Portland's oldest restaurants, with a great happy hour and walls crammed with Old Portland memorabilia. At the corner of Ankeny and Southwest Third Avenue is the tourist favorite ❺ **Voodoo Doughnut,** which will most likely have a huge line outside. Go ahead—we'll be in the alley.

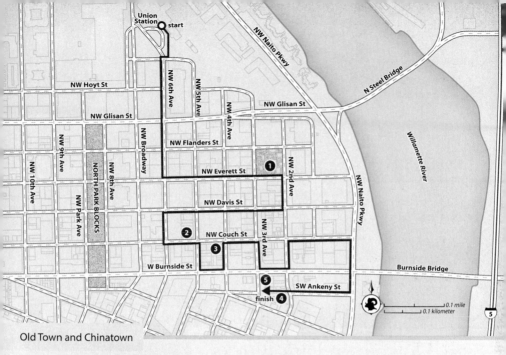

Old Town and Chinatown

Points of Interest

1. Lan Su Chinese Garden portlandchinesegarden.org, 239 NW Everett St., 503-228-8131
2. Ground Kontrol groundkontrol.com, 511 NW Couch St., 503-796-9364
3. Floating World Comics floatingworldcomics.com, 400 NW Couch St., 503-241-0227
4. Dan & Louis Oyster Bar danandlouis.com, 208 SW Ankeny St. Portland, 503-227-5906
5. Voodoo Doughnut voodoodoughnut.com, 22 SW Third Ave., 503-241-4704

2 Downtown Park Blocks
Museum Row

Above: Pioneer Courthouse Square

BOUNDARIES: SW Morrison St., SW 10th Ave., SW College St., SW Third Ave.
DISTANCE: 2 miles
DIFFICULTY: Easy
PARKING: Metered street parking
PUBLIC TRANSIT: Nearly any TriMet Bus or MAX light-rail line headed toward downtown

The area generally considered Downtown Portland encompasses a pretty vast stretch of territory, but for this walk we'll stick primarily to the South Park Blocks and surrounding area—basically the city's museum district. Not only is this where you'll find the art museum and history center, but it's also pleasantly removed from the bustling commercial parts of downtown. Most of the route goes along an inviting stretch of wide, traffic-free, tree-lined walkway leading toward the Portland State University campus. Before we get there, though, we'll explore the city's "living room," essentially the heart of downtown, or at least its people-watching capital: Pioneer Courthouse Square, a wide public gathering space often filled with downtown workers scarfing lunches bought from nearby food carts. It acts as an open-air event space, too, hosting concerts in summer, a farmers market each week, annual seasonal beer fests, ethnic food and culture fairs, protests and demonstrations, book sales, and, around December, the city's enormous holiday tree.

Walk Description

Start the walk at Pioneer Courthouse Square. Horrifyingly, the square was almost turned into an 11-story parking garage instead; that's what the owners of next-door department store Meier & Frank wanted to do with the space in the 1960s, but luckily the city refused to allow it. In fact, the threat of losing an opportunity for a shared public space downtown led Portland's leaders to start developing an actual city plan, and the creation of the public square was set into motion. It opened on April 6, 1984. Today it's the site of all kinds of civic activity, everything from farmers markets and food festivals to political protest rallies to jam-packed live music concerts. Its curved steps make a great place to sit and people-watch; the street theater here is tops.

Among the square's many features is also one of Portland's most photographed landmarks, *Allow Me*, J. Seward Johnson's bronze statue of a man holding out his umbrella. Under the water fountain below Starbucks—Portland's first, opened in 1989—is the ❶ **Travel Portland Visitor Information Center.** The arched wrought-iron gate at the opposite end of the square was originally part of the Hotel Portland (see Backstory on page 13). Beyond the gate and across the street is the historic Pioneer Courthouse, which opened in 1875 and serves the U.S. Courts' 9th Circuit.

Take Southwest Yamhill Street one block to Southwest Park Avenue and turn left. At Southwest Salmon Street turn left again, then turn right onto Southwest Broadway. This block is dominated by the ❷ **Arlene Schnitzer Concert Hall** and its epic neon PORTLAND sign, which used to read PARAMOUNT. (If you hesitate to walk underneath it, your fears are not unfounded: in the mid-1980s, the PARAMOUNT sign fell to the street during a disassembly and was replaced with the current PORTLAND sign). The Schnitz, as it's called, is the home of the Oregon Symphony and several other performing-arts groups. Originally a vaudeville hall, then a movie house (the Paramount), then a concert venue, it's now a great place to see just about any performance. The ornate Italian Rococo Revival interior and romantic lighting make even the most mundane lecture seem fancy.

Turn right up Southwest Main Street and then left on Park Avenue to reach ❸ **The Oregon Historical Society.** In addition to a stellar Oregon history–themed bookshop and an extensive archive of photos, maps, and documents, the OHS is also a museum with exhibits about various periods from the state's history. Objects and artifacts on display include Oregon's first car, the

Benson auto, cobbled together in a garage in 1904; meeting minutes from the earliest days of the Emanuel Hospital board, written in Swedish; and a massive guest book from the Lewis and Clark Centennial Expo in 1905 (so huge it gets wheeled around in its own custom-made transporter box). There's also a gallery of Northwest art, an exploration of the state's geology, and temporary exhibits.

Across the South Park Blocks from the OHS is the ❹ **Portland Art Museum.** PAM was founded in 1892; by 1913 it had gained enough traction to be one of the stops on the tour of the New York Armory Show, which rocked the art world of the time. The museum complex includes a number of buildings and galleries, as well as the Northwest Film Center. Don't neglect to seek out the museum's collection of graphic arts, which includes 30 prints donated by Robert Rauschenberg in 1976. (Rauschenberg's son, Christopher, is a photographer who lives in the area and is an active figure in the arts community, having cofounded two Portland galleries himself.) The Northwest Film Center schedule is also worth checking; its programs often include hard-to-find films, sometimes with director Q&As afterward, and the theater is pristine. The film center runs the hugely popular annual Portland International Film Festival each winter.

After you've left the museum, take the opportunity to stroll all the way to the end of the South Park Blocks. When the pedestrian walkway peters out toward the far side of the Portland State campus, make two lefts to cross to the other side of the South Park Blocks and come back toward town, staying on Southwest Park Avenue. At Southwest Market Street, turn right, then turn left at Southwest Third Avenue to swing by the Ira Keller Fountain, the centerpiece of Keller Fountain Park. It's a great place to hang out on a hot day; the intersecting planes of the waterfall are Tetris-level entrancing, and it's tucked away just enough off the main drag to feel like an escape from downtown traffic.

Follow Southwest Third Avenue to Main Street and turn left to walk between Lownsdale Square and Chapman Square; this was the nexus of Portland's Occupy Wall Street movement. Folks were camped out here for weeks during the protests of summer 2012, but eventually city authorities forced them to leave.

Also on Southwest Main Street, between Third and Fourth Avenues, is the Thompson elk fountain, which as anyone can see is facing the wrong direction, with its back to the oncoming cars, bikes, and buses. It has stood here since 1900, when, presumably, traffic was a little less streamlined.

Ahead of you on the left side of Main Street—and possibly the object of the Thompson Elk's disapproving gaze—is the much-maligned ❺ **Portland Building.** It holds city offices and meeting rooms, and it looks like a really big Christmas present nobody wants to find under the tree. (This opinion isn't terribly controversial; the Portland Building served as the lead example in a 2009 *Travel + Leisure* article titled "World's Ugliest Buildings," if that tells you anything.) Designed

Backstory: Hotel Portland

Though it would eventually become known as the most fabulous building ever to grace the city, the Hotel Portland had a troubled start. It was dreamed up in 1882 by Henry Villard, the railroad boss who built Union Station and is generally credited with getting a transcontinental rail line to Portland. But Villard went broke and high-tailed it back to his native Germany before the hotel could be finished. It took a couple of years and about 150 other investors, including William S. Ladd, Henry Failing, George Markle, and Henry Corbett, to wrap up construction on the project. The total cost was over $1 million.

The Hotel Portland (or Portland Hotel, depending on which antique postcard you're looking at) finally opened in 1890 and was by all accounts very posh, if a bit on the sturdy-and-stodgy side. It quickly became the cultural centerpiece of the city, with its elegant dining rooms and ballrooms. Eleven US presidents stayed there.

But its glory had begun to fade by the 1940s, when Meier & Frank bought the building; it was torn down in 1951 for parking space, which was eventually replaced by Pioneer Courthouse Square. The original wrought-iron gate from the hotel now stands at one end of the square.

by Michael Graves and opened in 1982, it is usually considered the first major postmodern building in the country. Perched over the front entrance is the (much more attractive, if also a bit intimidating) bronze statue *Portlandia,* by Raymond Kaskey. His design was selected by a committee, which included Graves, to complement the building's design. After the Statue of Liberty, *Portlandia* is the largest hammered-copper statue in the United States. If she stood up from her perch, she'd be the 50-Foot Woman. (Even crouched, she's 36 feet tall.) *Portlandia* traveled to her current location by barge along the Willamette River and was installed in 1985. (A few years later, local developer Joseph Weston offered to pay with his own money to have the statue moved to Waterfront Park, where people could see it without, as he put it, worrying about being hit by a bus, but the city declined his offer.)

Take Southwest Main Street to Southwest Fifth Avenue and turn right. Follow Fifth Avenue to Southwest Yamhill Street and turn left to return to Pioneer Courthouse Square.

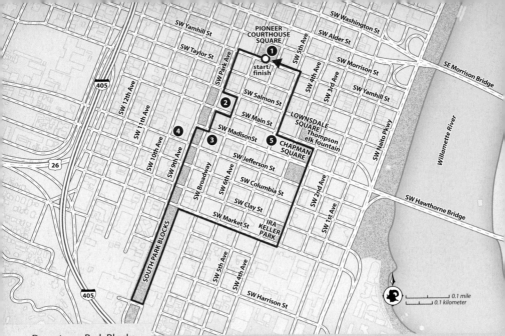

Downtown Park Blocks

Points of Interest

1. **Travel Portland Visitor Information Center** travelportland.com, 701 SW Sixth Ave., 503-275-8355
2. **Arlene Schnitzer Concert Hall** pcpa.com/schnitzer, 1037 SW Broadway, 503-248-4335
3. **The Oregon Historical Society** ohs.org, 1200 SW Park Ave., 503-222-1741
4. **Portland Art Museum** pam.org, 1219 SW Park Ave., 503-226-2811
5. **Portland Building** 1120 SW Fifth Ave.

3 Pearl District
Urban Art Project

Above: The main entrance of a Portland mainstay

BOUNDARIES: NW Lovejoy St., NW Couch St., NW 15th Ave., NW Broadway
DISTANCE: 2 miles
DIFFICULTY: Easy
PARKING: On street
PUBLIC TRANSIT: TriMet Bus 20 (W. Burnside and NW Park Ave.) or Portland Streetcar (NW 11th Ave. and Couch St., NW 11th Ave. and Glisan St.)

The Pearl District hasn't always been the urban designer's dream zone it is today. Until about 20 years or so ago, it wasn't really known as anything at all—sort of a blank, vaguely forbidding area between downtown and Northwest 23rd Avenue, full of empty warehouses and vacant lots. Gradually, a small vanguard of artists, drawn as ever by the cheap rent in out-of-the-way loft spaces, started moving in. Around the same time (roughly, the late 1980s and early 1990s), the Portland Development Commission noticed the area—the smart money always follows the artists. By 2000 the Pearl District had officially become a project. In October 2001 the City Council voted to adopt the Pearl District Development Plan: A Future Vision for a Neighborhood in Transition.

And boy, did that ever work. These days the Pearl is the kind of neighborhood you have to get dressed up for. Those empty warehouses are now sleekly renovated lofts and condos, and the streets are lined with upscale galleries, home-decor shops, and high-end restaurants. The Portland Streetcar carries people in from downtown (although it's often faster just to walk). Once a month the district becomes a huge street party during the First Thursday Art Walk, when galleries open their doors to premiere new exhibits. (Some people do actually go to look at the art, though many are there to check each other out—and for the free wine.) Some locals love to hate the Pearl—it's too moneyed and too polished to be interesting, and rent is way beyond a struggling artist's budget—but certainly from an urban-planning perspective, the transformation is remarkable.

Walk Description

Start the walk from Northwest 11th Avenue and Couch Street, where there's a Portland Streetcar stop. Walk east down Couch for a block, noting the rear entrance of Powell's Books on your right—don't worry, we'll come back to Powell's—then turn left on Northwest 10th Avenue.

In a courtyard between Northwest Everett and Flanders Streets, on your right, you'll find the installation of the two remaining Lovejoy Columns. These columns, which held up the ramp from Northwest Lovejoy Street onto the Broadway Bridge before it was demolished, were rescued by a hard-fought civic battle. Artist Tom Stefopoulos, who was a watchman at one of the nearby train yards in the 1940s, had embellished the columns during slow nights at work, and his paintings had become a favorite local landmark. When developers decided to tear down the Lovejoy Ramp in the late 1990s to make room for more of the Pearl, there was huge debate over what to do about the columns. For a while they lay in an empty lot, wrapped in tarps, awaiting their fate. Finally, developer John Carroll offered to install the two main columns in the plaza outside his Elizabeth Tower apartment building, and there they stand today. Whatever you make of the artwork, the inspired effort that went into preserving it—not to mention the awesome spectacle of those massive columns ripped free, their rebar guts exposed to the air—is damned impressive.

From Northwest 10th Avenue, turn left on Northwest Flanders Street, then right on Northwest 12th Avenue. If, like us, you're a sucker for fancy paper shops, stop in at ❶ Oblation Papers

& Press, on the right-hand side of the street. (Of course, there are galleries and shops throughout this area; let your curiosity guide you.)

At Northwest Hoyt Street, turn right. At Hoyt and Northwest 10th Avenue you'll find one of the few entirely unpretentious bars (maybe the only one?) in the Pearl—the ➋ **Low Brow Lounge.** It has somehow held out against the forces of commerce and fashion, sticking to its supercheap guns. It's impenetrably dark when you first walk in, but you'll adjust. Once you do, look around for the tiny "makeout booth" in the far corner. Plus: black lights!

Continue along Northwest Hoyt Street and, at Northwest Ninth Avenue, turn left to pass behind the ➌ **Ecotrust Building** (corner of Ninth and Northwest Johnson Street). Turn left on Northwest Johnson Street. The Ecotrust Building, formally known as the Jean Vollum Natural Capital Center, is a 100-year-old warehouse that was among the first in the area to be transformed into something new. When its remodel was finished in 2001, the U.S. Green Building Center gave it a LEED Gold rating, the first ever for a restoration of a historic building. Its design, which even those indifferent to architecture can appreciate, preserves the look and texture of the original (including some of the walls around the parking area, rough edges and all) and includes an ecoroof and a set of solar panels that provide a percentage of the building's energy supply. In short, it's a pretty cool building and one of the reasons people got so excited about what was going on in the Pearl District when the wave of warehouse renovations began. (There's also a really good pizza joint inside: ➍ **Hotlips,** which uses all-local organic ingredients.)

From Northwest Johnson Street, take a right on Northwest 10th Avenue, then a left on Northwest Kearney Street, to reach Jamison Square Park. When the park first appeared it was a little, um, stark: essentially a featureless concrete disc with a fountain in the middle. But it quickly grew into itself and now feels more like an urban oasis, with shade trees and seating areas around the fountain. It's wildly popular, especially with the parents of little kids, so it can get hectic on weekends and summer afternoons. But it definitely helps make the neighborhood seem like a place where people actually live, rather than just a theoretical exercise in how one might live. (The park is named after William Jamison, a universally adored Portland art gallery owner who died in 1995.)

Cross the square diagonally, emerging at Northwest 11th Avenue and Northwest Johnson Street, and take a right onto Johnson. At Northwest 13th Avenue turn left. This strip has a number of very highly rated restaurants, if you're feeling peckish. And for the coffee addicts, between Northwest Hoyt and Glisan is ➎ **Barista,** where you can get an impeccably pulled espresso shot and great advice on choosing a bag of beans to take home with you.

Between Everett and Davis on Northwest 13th Avenue is the Portland headquarters of the ➏ **Wieden + Kennedy** ad agency, which runs prominent campaigns for Nike and Old Spice,

Backstory: Esther Lovejoy

An early example of a tough Portland woman, Esther Lovejoy got a medical degree at the University of Oregon in 1894, graduating with honors. She married and had a son with a fellow med-school student, but both the son and the husband had died by 1911. Esther went on to marry a local businessman, George Lovejoy, but they were divorced in 1920. Before all of that, though, Portland's mayor appointed Esther to the city board of health. Two years later she became city health officer, the first woman to have such a major civic role in any large US city. She made it a priority to crack down on poor hygiene, particularly in schools and in terms of the city's garbage-collection practices, and she emphasized good-quality food and milk. She was also a fierce advocate for women's right to control their own lives; among other things, this included advocating for the right to vote. Oregon women achieved suffrage in 1912, but Esther didn't stop there; she continued to organize and fight for the right to vote on a national level. She wrote and published several books about the history of women in medicine. She also worked for public health improvements in poor and neglected areas overseas. She served as director of the international relief organization American Women's Hospitals from 1919 until she died in 1967.

among others. The building is yet another astounding renovation of an old warehouse (1908). Even the front doors are intimidating.

From Northwest 13th, turn left on West Burnside Street. This area was once home to the Henry Weinhard Brewery blocks. (Note the slick, newish Henry's 12th Street Tavern, a block down.) Weinhard ran a beer empire from here for decades. He made so much beer and distributed it so widely that at one point he supposedly offered to just go ahead and pump the lager directly into Skidmore Fountain so everybody could have some. The brewery produced 100,000 barrels of beer a year in 1890. And, remarkably, it survived Prohibition, temporarily adapting to the times with "near beer." But nothing lasts forever: in 1979, what was by then Blitz-Weinhard was sold to Pabst, and Pabst sold it to Stroh's in 1996. Three years later Stroh's sold the brand to Miller Brewing Co., and that was the end of Weinhard's brewing in the brewery blocks. (Henry Weinhard's beer is still made today, but in the Olympia Brewery in Tumwater, Washington.)

Follow West Burnside Street a few more blocks to Northwest 10th Avenue and the main entrance of ❼ **Powell's City of Books.** As you'll know from having just seen the back side of it, the place is massive—a whole city block and multiple levels of new, used, and rare books and magazines. Go on in and plan to stay a while. (Powell's also has regular author readings—check its website for a schedule.)

After you leave Powell's, continue along West Burnside Street and turn left on Northwest Ninth Avenue. This stretch includes another series of art galleries to explore. At Northwest Glisan Street, turn right, then right again on Northwest Eighth Avenue to walk along the North Park Blocks. Between Northwest Davis and Couch Streets is another building containing several of Portland's most important and influential galleries.

At the far end of the North Park Blocks, between Northwest Couch and West Burnside Streets, is a 12-foot bronze sculpture of an elephant carrying a smaller elephant on its back. This is a gift from a Chinese businessman whose bronze foundry is licensed to reproduce Chinese antiquities. The elephant is modeled after a much-smaller Shang dynasty wine pitcher. (No wine inside this one, though.)

From here, return to West Burnside Street, where you can catch a bus or walk a few blocks farther to downtown.

Hotlips pizzeria, located in the restored Ecotrust Building

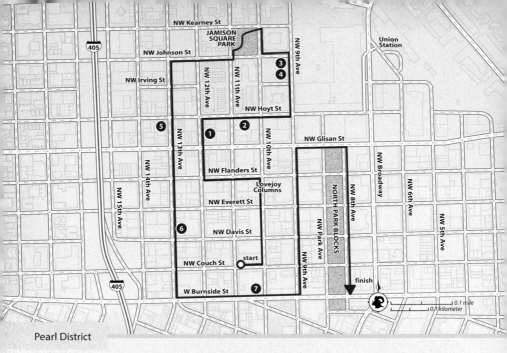

Pearl District

Points of Interest

1 Oblation Papers & Press oblationpapers.com, 516 NW 12th Ave., 503-223-1093

2 Low Brow Lounge 1036 NW Hoyt St., 503-226-0200

3 Ecotrust Building 721 NW Ninth Ave.

4 Hotlips hotlipspizza.com, NW 10th Ave. and Irving St., 503-595-2342

5 Barista baristapdx.com, 539 NW 13th Ave.

6 Wieden + Kennedy wk.com, 224 NW 13th Ave., 503-937-7000

7 Powell's City of Books powells.com, 1005 W. Burnside St., 503-228-4651

4 Northwest 21st and 23rd Avenues
Faded Glamour

Above: Shop for local and global gourmet grocery items at City Market NW.

BOUNDARIES: W. Burnside St., NW Raleigh St., NW 20th Ave., NW 24th Ave.
DISTANCE: 2 miles
DIFFICULTY: Easy
PARKING: Free street parking (with time limits)
PUBLIC TRANSIT: TriMet Bus 20 (W. Burnside St. and NW King Ave.)

Northwest (the general term for 21st and 23rd Avenues and the surrounding blocks) has seen easier times. Once considered the fanciest and most desirable part of Portland, it's now frequently mocked (Northwest 23rd has long sported the obvious nickname "Trendy-third") by people who live on the other side of the river; the glam boutiques and upscale restaurants that defined it went out of style or out of business as unemployment grew and disposable income shrank. For years this was the undebated first stop for any serious eating, drinking, or shopping to be done in Portland, but as the city has matured and other neighborhoods have taken over as talked-up destinations, Northwest has seemed to fade a little. In urban-planning magazine articles it's outshone by the neighboring Pearl District, and in youth-approved cool it loses out to Old Town, Alberta, and much of Southeast. Still, there's a lingering Euro-style beauty to the tree-lined streets and vintage buildings, and there are plenty of other reasons to seek out this area: one of the greatest art-house cinemas in the country, for one thing, not to mention a killer gourmet-grocery market, an appropriately cranky New York–style pizza joint, and several places in which one can sip a cocktail and feel like an adult. Plus the whole thing is part of the Alphabet Historic District, which is listed on the National Register of Historic Places and boasts some lovely residential buildings.

Walk Description

Start at the corner of West Burnside Street and Northwest 21st Avenue, heading north along 21st. The junior of the two main streets in Northwest is also the mellower one, with, generally speaking, more laid-back hangouts and fewer upscale shops.

If you duck down Northwest Glisan Street, to the right and two doors down, you'll come to the very pretty ❶ **Pope House Bourbon Lounge,** a bar inside a Victorian mansion that once housed the late, lamented Brazen Bean. (The Bean was a cocktail lounge of the sort that practically guaranteed your date would go well—it was one of the first cool, stylish places to get masterfully crafted grown-up cocktails in Portland.) The Pope House has a gorgeous outdoor garden for fair-weather seating, plus many shelves of whiskey, hardwood floors, and a rifle behind the bar inside. If you continue another block and a half along Northwest Glisan Street, you'll reach Couch Park, a nice little oasis named after Captain John Heard Couch, who owned most of the land in this part of town in the late 1800s.

Go back up Glisan to Northwest 21st Avenue and take a right. Just past Northwest Hoyt Street you'll come to ❷ **Cinema 21,** one of the best movie theaters left standing (in Portland or anywhere). It's a formerly single-screen theater from the 1960s that has since expanded and now shows top-notch art-house films; whatever it has on the marquee is always worth checking out (with the possible exception of *The Room,* the inexplicably popular *Rocky Horror*–like movie that screens here once a month and which inspired James Franco's biopic The Disaster Artist). Cinema 21 also frequently holds well-chosen revivals; examples have included a night of Bogart classics, several days of second-tier but still great film-noir titles, and a week or so of Hitchcock movies—in 35 mm, of course. And it's the headquarters for a number of local and regional film

You'll pass venerable dive bar Joe's Cellar on Northwest Pettygrove Street.

festivals. Seats are super comfy, and beer and wine are available.

Continuing along Northwest 21st Avenue, you'll find an ever-shifting lineup of restaurants and bars, some of which have been around forever (❸ **The 21st Avenue Bar & Grill,** with the unlikeliest of secret gardens on its lovely back patio) and many that will have vanished and reappeared in another incarnation by the time this book hits shelves (RIP, the Gypsy). One of the best choices is ❹ **Muu-Muu's,** next door to Cinema 21, for good food and drinks in a cozy, only slightly kitschy atmosphere.

Just past Northwest Johnson Street, on the left, is the ❺ **Russo Lee Gallery.** Laura Russo died in 2010, but the gallery, established in 1986, continues to be an important fixture in the Portland art scene (after Russo died, her longtime assistant, Martha Lee, took over running the gallery and has continued its mission). Russo was a major player in bringing wider attention to some of the most important artists of the Pacific Northwest, and the gallery helped establish many of the region's big names, including Henk Pander, Lucinda Parker, Tom Cramer, and Mary Josephson. Stop in for an efficient lesson in the art of the region, past and present.

Continue along Northwest 21st Avenue. As you cross Northrup Street you'll pass ❻ **Paley's Place** on the right—it's consistently rated one of Portland's top restaurants. Chef Vitaly Paley also runs Headwaters, the prestigious restaurant inside the Heathman Hotel (see the Downtown Park Blocks walk, page 10).

A little farther along, at the corner of Northwest Pettygrove Street, is venerable dive bar Joe's Cellar, which has been here forever and looks it. Diagonally across the street is its polar opposite: a huge, gleaming, black-and-gray block of modern luxury apartments called Q21. The facade incorporates parts of the concrete warehouse that once stood here; it's a cool building, but it's also exactly what people mean when they talk about New Portland. (The building sits right across the street from one of the largest development projects in the city, known as the

Conway Master Plan and described in the Nicolai and Slabtown Walk, page 45. The short version: be prepared for lots of construction noise around here.)

Make a left on Pettygrove and walk two blocks to Northwest 23rd Avenue, then turn left again. Just past the corner, you'll see the huge, vividly pastel confection that is the **❼ New Renaissance Bookshop,** a new-age bookstore that bills itself as Portland's Conscious Living Store. Pick up a meditation calendar or some wind chimes, straighten out your chakras, or maybe have your aura decontaminated. Seriously, just *try* to be grouchy in here—it can't be done.

Continue walking south along Northwest 23rd Avenue. No matter what time of day it is, as you cross Kearney Street you'll probably see a massive line of people waiting in front of **❽ Salt & Straw,** a surprisingly divisive artisanal ice-cream shop. Flavors are seasonal and weird (bone marrow? hmm). People either love it madly or turn up their noses, but whether the latter is due to the strange-sounding flavors or Portland's troubled relationship with success is often unclear.

There are tons of interesting and horrible shops along Northwest 23rd, but one of the most longstanding and worth poking around in is **❾ 3 Monkeys,** between Northwest Kearney and Johnson Streets. It sells funky clothes, jewelry, gifts, accessories, and knickknacks of all kinds. Farther along, between Northwest Flanders and Everett Streets, are a handful of kitchen and home-furnishing shops.

Between Northwest Irving and Hoyt Streets is the excellent **❿ Escape From New York Pizza,** the first (and for some, the only) by-the-slice pizza place in Portland. Escape From New York churns out classic thin-crust pie with attitude: service is usually grumpy, there aren't many choices, and they won't give you ranch dressing. (Why would you ask for ranch dressing?) Get a slice, fold it, walk around. Forget you ever even heard of New Renaissance Bookshop.

At West Burnside Street, hang a left for a couple of blocks until you reach **⓫ RingSide Steakhouse.** Even if you're stuffed with New York pizza, it's worth stopping in here for an artfully poured cocktail at the tiny, sunken bar. The RingSide is old-school Portland: a classy but not stuffy steakhouse with flawless service and an unbelievable happy-hour menu (even on Sundays). The place has been here since 1944 but underwent a thorough remodel in 2010, leaving all the charming touches (like a crooked fireplace) unchanged but adding kitchen space and a 10,000-square-foot wine cellar in the basement.

The bus stop where your walk began is right across the street.

Northwest 21st and 23rd Avenues

Points of Interest

1. Pope House Bourbon Lounge popehouselounge.com, 2075 NW Glisan St., 503-222-1056
2. Cinema 21 cinema21.com, 616 NW 21st Ave., 503-223-4515
3. 21st Avenue Bar & Grill 21stbarandgrill.com, 721 NW 21st Ave., 503-222-4121
4. Muu-Muu's muumuus.net, 612 NW 21st Ave., 503-223-8196
5. Russo Lee Gallery russoleegallery.com, 805 NW 21st Ave., 503-226-2754
6. Paley's Place paleysplace.net, 1204 NW 21st Ave., 503-243-2403
7. New Renaissance Bookshop newrenbooks.com, 1338 NW 23rd Ave., 503-224-4929
8. Salt & Straw saltandstraw.com, 838 NW 23rd Ave., 971-271-8168
9. 3 Monkeys 811 NW 23rd Ave., 503-222-5160
10. Escape From New York Pizza efnypizza.net, 622 NW 23rd Ave., 503-227-5423
11. RingSide Steakhouse ringsidesteakhouse.com, 2165 W. Burnside St., 503-223-1513

5 Goose Hollow
This Bud's for You

Above: Southwest Park Place leads to a garden housing the Lewis and Clark Memorial.

BOUNDARIES: I-405, W. Burnside St., SW Jefferson St., Washington Park
DISTANCE: 2 miles
DIFFICULTY: Moderate–strenuous (hilly in places)
PARKING: Free street parking
PUBLIC TRANSIT: TriMet Bus 15 (SW Morrison St. and 16th Ave.), MAX Red and Blue Lines
  (Providence Park Station)

Goose Hollow as an entity actually predates incorporated Portland by about six years. Daniel Lownsdale, who built the first house here, ran a tannery on the site that became Civic Stadium (now Providence Park, home of the beloved Portland Timbers major-league soccer team and the Portland Thorns FC, of the National Women's Soccer League). Years later, the area was named for the flocks of geese that used to roam around here—although you'd be forgiven for thinking it's because of the cozy and well-loved Goose Hollow Inn, the pub that former mayor Bud Clark has owned here since 1967. When Clark first opened the place, the neighborhood hadn't quite established a strong sense of identity, so Clark gave his pub a historical name in hopes of reviving the Goose Hollow spirit. This apparently worked like a charm, as the name has stuck since the 1970s and the neighborhood seems to have coalesced around it.

Walk Description

Start at Southwest Morrison Street and 18th Avenue, at the corner of ❶ Providence Park. Walk up Morrison Street alongside the stadium. At Southwest 20th Avenue, turn left—but not before taking note of the remarkably disturbing happy-face bronze sculpture at the corner, one of a matched pair, presumably intended to keep the faint of heart from entering the stadium to watch a game.

On your left as you walk up the hill, you have a chance to peer down at folks in the exclusive Multnomah Athletic Club doing their workouts. (Hey, if they didn't want anyone to look, they wouldn't have put windows there.) Turn right on Southwest Salmon Street, then right again briefly on Southwest King Avenue; then make a quick left onto Southwest Park Place. The houses up here are enormous and beautiful, with tons of character.

Continue up Southwest Park Place all the way to the point at which it dead-ends in stairs leading up to a garden and the Lewis and Clark Memorial, a granite column commissioned in 1902; President Teddy Roosevelt laid its first cornerstone in 1903. If you're so inclined, you can continue along this path to reach the Washington Park International Rose Test Garden. (And, if you like, you could also link up with the Washington Park walk, page 31.) It's a bit of a climb to get up the stairs, but you're rewarded with an amazing view from the top. If you're tired, simply climb as many stairs as you feel like, have a look around, and head back along the other side of Southwest Park Place the way you came.

At Southwest Vista Avenue, turn right. This leads to the Vista Bridge, an underrated Portland viewpoint. The bridge, which stretches over busy Southwest Jefferson Street and the MAX light-rail tracks heading west toward Hillsboro, is rather morbidly nicknamed the Suicide Bridge due to the number of people who've jumped from it. Even so, the view from the middle of the bridge is fantastic, especially at sunset, and the little details of the bridge's embellishments—gargoyles, lanterns, iron spires—add a Gothic touch.

Cross back over the bridge and turn right on Southwest Kings Court. This is a narrow one-way street, with traffic going the other way, so be alert—but don't miss the yard filled entirely with a whispering forest of bamboo plants, on your left as you start down the hill. Toward the

Backstory: Bud Clark, The People's Mayor

Bud Clark was just a folksy tavern owner when he ran for mayor against incumbent Frank Ivancie in 1984. Ivancie was a former city commissioner, a formidable and well-connected career politician who had already secured endorsements from many of the city's most powerful groups and institutions, including labor unions and *The Oregonian*. (Trivia: It was Ivancie who, as part of his 1982 "war on crime" agenda, tried to make it illegal to give Portland police officers the middle finger, according to *Willamette Week*.) Clark, on the other hand, was known mainly for having flashed a statue of a nude woman in the now-iconic "Expose Yourself to Art" poster. It should've been a joke of a campaign, and that's more or less how Ivancie's people decided to treat it. But against the odds, and most observers' predictions, Clark won—by a wide margin—thanks in large part to his grassroots campaigning and his folksy, man-of-the-people style.

Clark served as mayor for eight years. His accomplishments while in office included formulating the city's first-ever 12-point plan for tackling homelessness; leading development of the Oregon Convention Center; introducing the city to community policing; and sponsoring the Mayor's Ball, a fund-raising live music concert that had the pleasing side effect of helping to solidify the indie music scene in Portland. Today one of the city's primary transitional housing and community resource centers for the homeless is named Bud Clark Commons in honor of the former mayor. This walk takes in some of his stomping grounds and, of course, his excellent pub.

bottom of the hill, just before Kings Court swerves left to become Southwest King Avenue, a small concrete footpath leads off to the right, down a hill between two houses. Follow its zigzag pattern to the bottom of the hill, emerging at Southwest Jefferson Street, and hang a left on Jefferson.

At the corner of Southwest 19th Avenue and Jefferson Street is the ❷ Goose Hollow Inn, run by former mayor Bud Clark (who can still occasionally be seen hanging out there). It's an extremely cozy little pub, with a great wooden deck, friendly servers, hearty pizza, and a famously good Reuben sandwich.

Where Southwest Jefferson Street meets Southwest 18th Avenue, turn left. Along Southwest 18th between Main and Salmon Streets, watch the sidewalk for a local celebrity signature: a drawing of Bart Simpson etched into the concrete. *Simpsons* creator Matt Groening graduated from nearby Lincoln High School in 1972. The sidewalk art was actually drawn (with Groening's permission, of course) by Portland artist Matt Wuerker as part of a public art project that coincided with the building of the new light-rail line through Goose Hollow.

Follow Southwest 18th Avenue to the stoplight at Southwest Salmon Street and cross, turning right on Salmon.

At Southwest 15th Avenue, turn left. Just past Southwest Yamhill Street you'll come to the Hotel deLuxe, formerly the Mallory, a very nicely renovated boutique hotel whose tiny 1950s-style bar, the ❸ Driftwood Room, is a cocktail connoisseur's dream. The snappily dressed folks behind the bar work magic here—put yourself in their tender care, and you won't regret it. (Plenty of others are in on the secret, though, and the bar is really small, so it's best to come on a weeknight or right when the place opens.)

The walk ends here; catch MAX light rail just around the corner, on either Southwest Yamhill or Southwest Morrison, depending on which way you're heading. (It's also a short, easy walk from here to the Fifth Avenue–Sixth Avenue Transit Mall downtown.)

Goose Hollow Inn, a classic Portland tavern since 1967

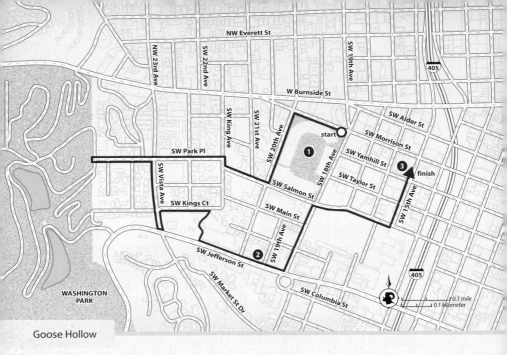

Goose Hollow

Points of Interest

① Providence Park providenceparkpdx.com, SE Morrison St. and 18th Ave.

② Goose Hollow Inn goosehollowinn.com, 1927 SW Jefferson St., 503-228-7010

③ Driftwood Room hoteldeluxeportland.com/food-drink, 729 SW 15th Ave., 503-384-2347

Inside the stadium at Providence Park

6 Washington Park
Lions, Toddlers, and Trees

Above: The International Rose Test Garden boasts more than 600 types of roses.

BOUNDARIES: W. Burnside St., SW Vista Ave., SW Sunset Hwy., SW Skyline Blvd.
DISTANCE: 3 miles, with options to extend
DIFFICULTY: Easy–moderate
PARKING: In lots (some with a fee)
PUBLIC TRANSIT: MAX Red and Blue Lines (Washington Park Station), TriMet Bus 63
  (SW Kingston Ave. and Japanese Garden)

Yet another of the many things that make Portlanders feel so lucky to live here: this hilltop park complex practically right in the middle of town features a network of wilderness trails linking a huge range of family-friendly things to see and do, not to mention postcard-quality views in all directions. This is Washington Park, the Southwest Portland companion to the adjoining (and somewhat wilder) Forest Park, an awesome 5,000-acre forested woodland that occupies a large part of Northwest Portland. Best of all, Washington Park is easy to get to: just hop on MAX light rail, take an elevator up to the surface, and you're standing in the midst of a handful of attractions, including several good museums and the Oregon Zoo. From there it's a short hike along softly winding forest paths to reach a pair of beautifully sculpted gardens. You'll want to bring snacks or a picnic for this walk, if only because you'll have an excuse to linger.

Walk Description

Start at the Washington Park MAX Station, which is 260 feet underground. An elevator takes you up to surface level, more or less in the parking lot of the zoo.

The ❶ Oregon Zoo has been in its current location since the late 1950s. It's probably most famous (at least locally) for being the home of Packy, the Asian elephant, part of the zoo's successful elephant-breeding program. (Packy, who died in 2017 at age 54, was the first elephant born in the Western Hemisphere in more than 40 years.) The zoo also holds a popular series of outdoor music concerts in the summer, and in December there are elaborate animatronic displays of holiday lights.

From the zoo entrance, loop around the parking lot to reach the ❷ Portland Children's Museum. Recommended mostly for very young kids (under 5 years old or so), this is a safe place to turn your toddlers loose on a rainy day and let them run around from one hands-on creative-learning exhibit to the next—they can dig holes, buy groceries, finger paint, and so on. Kids can also attend vacation camps and group classes (in science, painting, yoga, and one that's all about making messes). The museum does get crammed on the weekends, and if you don't relish the idea of being in a room full of giggling, screaming, scampering tots, you might want to skip this one, but parents seem to love it.

Continuing around the parking lot to your left, you'll come to the ❸ World Forestry Center, another kid-friendly museum, this one dedicated to understanding the value of forests in everyday life. Its exhibits cover forest use and preservation in various parts of the world, at levels that will interest kids but won't bore their parents. Outside stands a massive petrified stump from a giant Sequoia tree that's 5 million years old.

Turn left on exiting the World Forestry Center, and follow the trail to the entrance of the Vietnam Veterans of Oregon Memorial. Dedicated in 1987, it lists the names of Oregon veterans who served in the war, as well as relevant background stories and random events from around the state that were occurring at the same time. The memorial is situated in a shallow, grass-covered hollow; sections of the wall are distributed along a paved spiral sidewalk, which leads you gently up to the edge of the bowl and connects with the Wildwood Trail.

The network of trails in Washington Park connects a variety of attractions.

Follow the spiral pathway from the memorial until it joins the Wildwood Trail. From here, you'll stay on the Wildwood to reach Hoyt Arboretum; the trail is well signposted, so it shouldn't be difficult to follow. This is a great place to be on a hot summer day, as the deep woods surrounding the trail provide plenty of cool shade. Veer left at the spur trail to the arboretum (also clearly marked).

❹ **Hoyt Arboretum** is what it sounds like: a tree museum, spread out across 187 acres, showcasing 1,100 species of trees from around the world. The most casual appraisal makes it clear that this area is prime real estate, and it was originally intended for residential development. But before that could happen, civic leaders lobbied to preserve the land as a public space on which to conserve unusual or endangered tree species. In 1922, Multnomah County gave the land to the city of Portland for the park that became the arboretum. It's named after Ralph Warren Hoyt, one of the county commissioners who pushed to have it established. If time and energy allow, the trails winding through the arboretum are worth exploring on your own—the trees make especially vivid scenery in fall and spring. The visitor center here has maps, brochures, guidebooks, and lots of other information on the park and Portland in general.

Backtrack from the arboretum entrance to return to the Wildwood Trail, and continue along the trail in the same direction you were heading before (roughly east). The trail through this section of forest makes a number of switchbacks, and there are a few intersections with other trails, but it's well marked. After about 1.7 miles, on some of the switchbacks you should be able to catch the occasional glimpse of the ❺ **Japanese Garden** below you.

In just under 2 miles you'll come to a spur trail off to the right that leads to the Japanese Garden. Established as part of Portland's sister-city relationship with Sapporo, Japan, the garden opened in 1967. The design incorporates several different interconnected garden zones, each with its own mood, including the Strolling Pond Garden, the Tea Garden, the Natural Garden, the Flat Garden, and the Sand and Stone Garden. A 2017 expansion designed by Japanese architect Kengo Kuma added 3.4 acres to the garden, including new LEED-certified buildings to house gallery space, workshops, and a café. The traditional tea house occasionally hosts formal tea ceremonies and one-off food-focused events, such as sake and sushi tastings. An incredibly pretty, calming place, it's best on an overcast day (not difficult to achieve in Portland), when the lush green ferns and stone sculptures seem to glow. Tours are available daily; check the website for details, or ask at the ticket office.

Exit the garden and cross the large parking lot at Southwest Kingston Avenue to enter the ❻ International Rose Test Garden. You'll recognize it from the millions of postcard snapshots that have been taken from here. The rose garden, like the rest of Washington Park, is a great place to wander idly, sniffing and looking at the unbelievable variety of roses in their tidy arrangements. There are supposedly 9,525 rose bushes here, representing 610 different types. This is also (understandably) a popular wedding spot. The garden is maintained by the Portland Rose Society, a nonprofit that has been around since the 1800s; it was established by the Pittock family, they of the mansion just over the next ridge, in Forest Park. (You can get a closer look at the Pittock Mansion on Walk 7: Forest Park). As you wander, don't miss the Frank L. Beach Memorial Fountain, designed by Lee Kelly in 1974 in honor of the man who gave Portland its "City of Roses" nickname. TriMet's bus 63 stops in front of the rose garden.

Vietnam Veterans of Oregon Memorial

Washington Park

Points of Interest

1 Oregon Zoo oregonzoo.org, 4001 SW Canyon Rd., 503-226-1561

2 Portland Children's Museum portlandcm.org, 4015 SW Canyon Rd., 503-223-6500

3 World Forestry Center worldforestry.org, 4033 SW Canyon Rd., 503-228-1367

4 Hoyt Arboretum hoytarboretum.org, 4000 SW Fairview Blvd., 503-865-8733

5 Japanese Garden japanesegarden.com, 611 SW Kingston Ave., 503-223-1321

6 International Rose Test Garden tinyurl.com/rosetestgarden, 850 SW Rose Garden Way, 503-823-3636

7 Forest Park
House on the Hill

Above: The Stone House, at the junction of the Wildwood and Lower Macleay Trails

BOUNDARIES: NW 29th Ave., NW Upshur St., Forest Park, NW Pittock Dr.
DISTANCE: 5 miles
DIFFICULTY: Moderate–strenuous
PARKING: Lot and street parking (both free)
PUBLIC TRANSIT: TriMet Bus 15 (numerous stops along NW Thurman St. near the park)

It would be crazy not to recommend a walk in Forest Park, the largest and one of the richest urban parks in the country. It's essentially a huge wilderness right in Portland's backyard: some 5,000 acres of untouched forest laced with well-maintained trails of all lengths and levels. And many of its entry points are, like this trek to the historic Pittock Mansion, incredibly easy to get to from the city. It sounds cliché, but it's true: within minutes you can feel like you're miles away from anything resembling pavement, trekking through deep dark woods with sunlight filtering through a canopy of trees. (Or, perhaps more realistic, a faint mist hanging in the gray air—but even bad weather looks pretty in the woods.) This hike's easily accessed entry points make it a popular choice, so it can get a little busy on weekends; go early in the morning or late in the afternoon to avoid the biggest crowds. But even on a crowded day, it's well worth sharing the trail to reach those incredible views at the top.

Walk Description

Start at the Lower Macleay Trailhead, where you'll find a small parking lot, restrooms, and a picnic table or two. Find it by following Northwest Thurman Street to 29th Avenue, then going down the hill and turning left on Upshur Street (signs can be a little tricky to spot).

From the parking lot, walk under the Thurman Street Bridge toward the red sculptures where the trail begins. You'll see a series of crumbling wooden structures on the left—this is where Balch Creek (which you'll follow for much of the walk) heads underground for a few miles on its way to the river. Balch Creek is named for Danford Balch, an early Oregon settler with quite a story. Balch and his family settled on 350 acres near Portland in 1850. In 1858, Balch's 16-year-old daughter, Anna, ran off with a ranch hand who went by the Gothic-literary name of Mortimer Stump (really). This did not go over well with old Danford. During the ensuing negotiations, tempers may have flared, and Danford Balch "accidentally" shot and killed Mortimer Stump. And that's how Balch became the first man sentenced to death and executed in Oregon (by hanging, in 1859). No word on how things turned out for his poor daughter.

At the second wooden bridge, peek over the railing into the pool—you can usually catch sight of some cutthroat trout hiding there. And if you have a keen eye, somewhere along the trail you might spot an owl lurking in the branches overhead.

In just under a mile, you'll reach the Stone House, a perfect little moss-covered gray stone cottage. It was built by the Works Progress Administration as a public restroom, believe it or not, and served as such until 1962, when a huge storm destroyed the plumbing system and the park service decided it would cost too much to fix. Note the sawed-off slices of log arrayed around the trail, and feel free to take a load off for a while if you're so inclined.

At the Stone House, the trail you're on divides—continue straight along the Wildwood Trail rather than turning right to go up the hill.

About half a mile later, you'll cross Cornell Road at a crosswalk—be very careful, as this section of road is the fun, curvy sort that tempts drivers to think they're questing on *Top Gear*. Continue uphill on the Wildwood Trail, along a fairly steep series of switchbacks. At a couple of places, the trail crosses the Upper Macleay Trail, but signs are clearly marked; just stay on the Wildwood, and any time you're in doubt, go uphill rather than down.

Backstory: Pittock Mansion

Though it doesn't look quite like what we typically imagine a pioneer home to be, Pittock Mansion is, in a way, a pioneer home, if a very decadent and sophisticated one. It was built for Henry and Georgiana Pittock, who traveled here from Pennsylvania along the Oregon Trail and lived in the mansion from 1914 to 1919. But this wasn't exactly their "starter" home.

Henry Pittock, born in England, arrived in Portland at age 19 in 1853, completely broke. At the time Portland had a population of about 1,500 people. Henry got a job at the then weekly *Oregonian* newspaper and slowly began to work his way up the paper's chain of command. Seven years later, he bought the whole enterprise and turned it into a daily. That same year, Henry met and married Georgiana Martin Burton, who'd arrived from Missouri with her parents a year after he had. When they married, she was only 15 years old. The couple quickly became socialites and civic leaders, participating in the annual Rose Festival parade, forming relief organizations for children in need and for working women, and so on. They had six kids and built up a wide range of business interests. In 1909 they started planning and designing their house on the hill. By the time they moved into the mansion, Georgiana was 68 and Henry was 80. Georgiana died in 1918 and Henry in 1919. The house has been owned by the city of Portland since 1964 and was opened to the public the following year.

You'll come out at the parking lot of the impressive ❶ **Pittock Mansion.** Completed in 1914, it was the home of Henry Pittock and his wife, Georgiana. The Pittocks arrived via the Oregon Trail, and Henry started work as a typesetter at the local paper. He worked his way up and eventually bought the newspaper, which he transformed into the daily *Oregonian*. You can take a tour of the mansion's interior ($11 per adult), with its 23 rooms decked out in period furnishings and modern-at-the-time features like electric lighting, central heating, and an elevator. But it's nice enough (and free) just to wander the grounds, appreciating the surrounding gardens and taking in the awesome views, including Mount Hood and, on a clear day, Mount St. Helens and three other Cascade peaks. If it's nice out, eat your lunch on the front lawn of the mansion.

Return to the parking lot the same way or, for something different, take a right onto the Upper Macleay Trail on your way down; it links back up with the Wildwood just above the Cornell Road crossing.

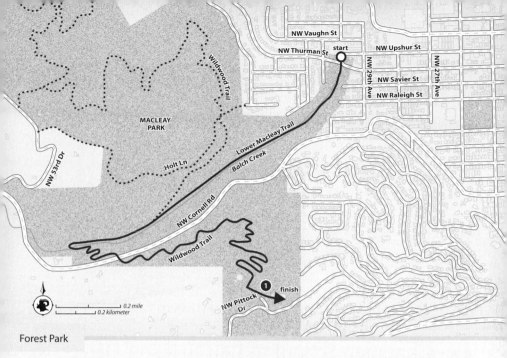

NW Vaughn St

NW Thurman St   start

NW Upshur St

NW 29th Ave

NW Savier St

NW Raleigh St

NW 27th Ave

Wildwood Trail

MACLEAY PARK

NW 53rd Dr

Holt Ln

Lower Macleay Trail

Balch Creek

NW Cornell Rd

Wildwood Trail

① → finish

NW Pittock Dr

0.2 mile

0.2 kilometer

Forest Park

Point of Interest

① **Pittock Mansion** pittockmansion.org, 3229 NW Pittock Dr., 503-823-3623

Lower Macleay Trail

8 Chapman School to Leif Erikson Drive
Swift Work

Above: Northwest Thurman Street

BOUNDARIES: NW Vaughn St., NW 23rd Ave., NW Overton St., NW Cornell Rd., Forest Park
DISTANCE: 2 miles, with option to extend
DIFFICULTY: Easy, with option for strenuous
PARKING: Free street parking
PUBLIC TRANSIT: TriMet Bus 15 (NW 25th Ave. and Thurman St.)

This walk, in an out-of-the-way little pocket of Portland, gives you the option for a longer hike into the forest at the end, depending on your stamina, interest, and fitness level. During late summer and fall, the route includes one of the city's most otherworldly and fascinating phenomena: the swooping and swirling bedtime rituals of the flock of Vaux's swifts that roost at Chapman Elementary School. (You can watch them most evenings from late August through September, depending on the weather and the restlessness of the birds. Until you've seen it, it's hard to appreciate what a cool thing this is, but trust us, it's worth the effort.)

Any time of year, this is a part of Northwest Portland that may not get much press but rewards exploration; one could describe it as polished industrial. Springing up along Thurman and Upshur Streets are the offices of creative-class types—graphic designers, architects, photographers, and video-production workers—mixed in with the comfortably established residential neighborhood full of old leafy trees, wooden bungalows, and shiny new apartment buildings. Looming over all of this is the landmark Montgomery Park office building, whose red-neon sign is visible from most parts of Portland. The proximity of regular folks, creative industrial workers, and untamed forest makes this area an appealing section of town to wander around in.

Walk Description

Start at the corner of Northwest 23rd Place (not 23rd Avenue) and Thurman Street, where you have no fewer than three fine choices for loading up on picnic supplies: ❶ St. Honoré Bakery, home of authentic French-style sandwiches and achingly beautiful pastries; ❷ Food Front Cooperative Grocery, a community-owned market of almost *Portlandia*-level earnestness, with organic produce and a gourmet deli; and ❸ Kenny & Zuke's Bagelworks, formerly Sandwichworks, where despite the name change you can still get some of the deli's famous hero sandwiches and grinders.

Having stocked up on edibles, head west up Northwest Thurman Street to Northwest 25th Avenue and turn left. In two blocks you'll reach the corner of the Wallace Dog Park, which you'll either love or hate depending on your canine-friendliness. (It's not just for dogs, of course, but they are a noticeable presence.) You can make your way diagonally across the park or walk its perimeter, along 25th Avenue, then turn right on Northwest Pettygrove Street.

Chapman Elementary School and its surrounding lawn are a popular destination in late summer and early fall, when a huge flock of Vaux's swifts roosts here and preps for the long migratory trip to Central America. Anywhere from 2,000 to 7,000 of the birds bed down for the night in the school's chimney, and about an hour before sunset they start swirling and swooping around the place in a massive, billowing cloud. It's hard to imagine they can possibly all fit inside the chimney, but they seem to have it figured out. The maneuvering flock is really impressive to watch; grab a spot on the lawn and see for yourself. Local Audubon Society volunteers are usually around to answer any questions you might have about the birds.

Cross the schoolyard to the right (east) and turn left on Northwest 26th Avenue. At the corner of Northwest 26th and Thurman you'll see the ❹ Friendly House, originally the Marshall Street Community Center, founded by the Presbyterian church in 1926. (It has been called the Friendly House since 1930.) It's a nonprofit social services organization whose role in the community took shape early on, when volunteers here helped families get through the economic struggles of the Great Depression. These days, the Friendly House looks out in particular for underserved populations, including LGBT senior citizens and the kids of homeless families. There's also a wide range of workshops and classes for adults (for example, art therapy for people recovering from domestic abuse, yoga for senior citizens, and fitness for people with mobility issues), as well as camps, field trips, and preschool and after-school programs for kids. The mosaic-tile sculpture out front was designed by Lynn Takata and put together by Friendly House volunteers and supporters in 2011.

This dirt-and-gravel road used by runners and cy stretches 11 miles into Forest Park.

Crossing Northwest Thurman Street, notice the tall, skinny, metallic bungalow at the corner. This is the home of ❺ *Tin House* magazine's Portland headquarters. (There are also offices in Brooklyn.) Yep, it's an actual tin house! If you haven't encountered the *Tin House* literary mag before, make a point of picking up the latest issue. There's also a newish book-publishing division, with a roster of critically acclaimed indie successes.. The publisher also holds an annual weeklong writers workshop each summer at Portland's Reed College campus (and a shorter one in winter at the Oregon Coast), with readings and lectures that are open to the public.

At Northwest Vaughn Street, turn left and walk toward 27th Avenue, where you'll be able to see the Montgomery Park Building and its huge red sign (lit up sort of fetchingly at night). Built in 1920, the structure was once part of Montgomery Ward's catalog business, part of the company's efforts to expand its mail-order markets westward, into the Pacific Northwest, Alaska, and Hawaii. At the time it was the largest commercial building in Portland (even before it was expanded in 1936). It was built on the site of the 1905 Lewis and Clark Centennial Exposition (see Backstory, opposite page). Montgomery Ward was here until the mid-1980s, when the company closed and sold the warehouse. Bought and renovated by the Naito family (who were reportedly pleased that they only had to change the *W* and the *D* in the sign), it now houses office buildings and trade-show space.

Backstory: 1905 Lewis and Clark Centennial Exposition

The summer and early fall of 1905 saw Portland's first and only world's fair, the Lewis and Clark Centennial Expo. Millions of people showed up, and many of them stayed; the city's population doubled in the next five years. World's fairs in general were a chance for people to see the very newest and most exciting advancements in architecture, science, technology, and ideas. Twenty-one countries participated in the Lewis and Clark Expo, each with an elaborately decorated pavilion meant to display its glorious bounty. Often the pavilions themselves *were* the display, as in the case of the Forest Building, which was made of huge Douglas-fir logs, bark and all, and meant to represent the potential of the logging industry in the Pacific Northwest. (It stayed up and in use until a fire destroyed it in 1964.) Many of the structures were later taken apart and moved to other parts of town when the Expo ended—for instance, the McMenamins theater pub in St. Johns and its original dome (see Walk 25: St. Johns and Cathedral Park for details).

Turn left on Northwest 27th Avenue, walk two blocks, and then turn right onto Northwest Thurman Street. At the corner is ❻ **Fat Tire Farm,** one of the earliest and best-liked bicycle shops in town. You can rent a mountain bike to go exploring in Forest Park, as well as pick up maps and get all kinds of advice on bike trails, commuting, repairs, and the bicycle community in Portland. Unlike a few other shops in town, the staff doesn't make you feel like an idiot if you don't already happen to be an expert cyclist—it's a good place to ask questions and find help without being intimidated.

Continue along Northwest Thurman Street through increasingly quiet blocks. Just past Northwest 29th Avenue you'll cross the bridge over Macleay Park, with stairs allowing you to drop down to the little park and picnic area where the Lower Macleay Trail begins (and where you could also link up with Walk 7: Forest Park). Otherwise, or after a picnic break, forge ahead on Northwest Thurman Street as it winds its way uphill and the houses and yards grow ever more attractive. At the end of the curvy street, you'll come to a gateway that marks the entrance to Northwest Leif Erikson Drive. (Sometimes also called Leif Erikson Trail, it was named Hillside Drive until 1933, when the local Sons of Norway lobbied to change the name in honor of the Norwegian explorer.) This trail is a nice wide dirt-and-gravel road that stretches 11 miles into Forest Park; it's a favorite among runners and bicyclists. We'll turn you loose here to decide for yourself how far you feel like going. (This trail is also a fine entry point for more-extensive hikes throughout Forest Park, but you'll definitely want to have a good map on hand.)

To return to the starting point, simply reverse course and follow Northwest Thurman Street to Northwest 23rd Place. Or hop Bus 15 back; you can catch it at Northwest Gordon Street.

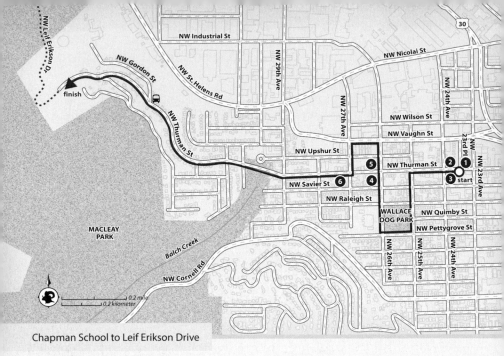

Chapman School to Leif Erikson Drive

Points of Interest

1. St. Honoré Bakery sainthonorebakery.com, 2335 NW Thurman St., 503-445-4342
2. Food Front Cooperative Grocery foodfront.coop, 2375 NW Thurman St., 503-222-5658
3. Kenny & Zuke's Bagelworks kzbagelworks.com, 2376 NW Thurman St., 503-954-1737
4. Friendly House friendlyhouseinc.org, 1737 NW 26th Ave., 503-228-4391
5. *Tin House* tinhouse.com, 2617 NW Thurman St.
6. Fat Tire Farm fattirefarm.com, 2714 NW Thurman St., 503-222-3276

9 Nicolai and Slabtown

Rough and Ready

Above: Admire the facade of the Smith Teamaker building before stopping for a cup.

BOUNDARIES: NW Front Ave., NW Nicolai St., NW 24th Ave., NW Lovejoy St.
DISTANCE: 3 miles
DIFFICULTY: Easy
PARKING: Free street parking; small lot near start/finish
PUBLIC TRANSIT: TriMet Bus 16 (NW Front Ave. and Nicolai St.)

This walk covers an odd little slice of Portland between the posh Northwest 23rd and 21st Avenues and the river, with the hard-core Industrial Northwest neighborhood to the north. It's a funky, gritty, and not always attractive mix of freight containers and warehouses, coffee laboratories and mysterious museums. It's also one of the few parts of Portland that still feel refreshingly rough around the edges, even as sleek new apartment buildings and upscale grocery stores gradually venture in.

The neighborhood overall has started to see massive and dramatic changes, thanks to what's generally called the Conway Master Plan—a long-term plan to develop 17.5 acres, mostly occupied by parking lots and warehouses, that were owned by local freight company Con-way. (In 2015 another company, XPO Logistics, bought Con-way for $3 billion, but the area and the plan have kept the original name, at least for now.) The plans for development include 2,500 new homes, some parks and public plaza-type spaces, a library, and a mix of retail, including upmarket grocery store New Seasons, whose opening in 2015 was the first of these projects to take shape. It's unclear how quickly the rest of the changes will happen, but it's already obvious that this neighborhood will be utterly transformed. Stay tuned!

Walk Description

Start your walk with some high-grade caffeine at ❶ **Ristretto Roasters,** a gorgeous coffee shop inside the restored ❷ **Schoolhouse Electric & Supply Co.** warehouse building at Northwest Nicolai Street and 22nd Avenue. You can get a pour-over and, at the same time, an aesthetically pleasing object lesson in what's been happening recently, architecture-wise, in the industrial and formerly industrial parts of Northwest Portland. (Schoolhouse Electric itself is pretty cool, too—browse its impressively restored 5,000-square-foot showroom for beautifully designed and redesigned lighting, luxurious textiles, rescued and repurposed furniture, hardware, fixtures, and more.)

Cross Northwest Nicolai Street and continue south along Northwest 22nd Avenue past empty shipping containers and random industrial equipment until you get to Northwest Wilson Street. Take a left on Wilson (although you may want to stop in at Motocorsa for a peek at some very shiny Italian motorcycles—it's a Ducati dealership, and quite fancy inside). From Wilson, hang a right onto Northwest 21st Avenue, then a left onto Northwest Vaughn Street. This might not be the most scenic part of Portland, but it's interesting from a behind-the-scenes point of view.

Follow Vaughn as it bends to the right; turn left at Northwest Upshur Street, and don't miss the scary metal sculpture of an angry bear (made of gears and metal scraps) in front of Castaway, a restored warehouse that now operates as an event space for everything from weddings to food and beverage festivals. From here you also have a cool view of the underside of the Fremont Bridge.

Take a right at Northwest 17th Avenue, then a left onto Northwest Thurman Street. You can stop here to pick up some charcuterie or have a sit-down lunch at ❸ **Olympia Provisions,** or admire the pretty facade of the Smith Teamaker building next door before popping in for a cuppa.

Continue along Northwest Thurman Street to the funky-looking Triangle Building, where you can get a coffee and pastry or a hearty meal worthy of a stevedore at ❹ **Breken Kitchen.** (The grilled cheese–and–tomato soup special is a particular favorite.) Take a right onto Northwest 15th Avenue, and follow it underneath the highway bridges. Continue along 15th, then turn left onto

Northwest Pettygrove Street and right onto Northwest 13th Avenue. At the corner of Northwest 13th and Marshall Street is among the first of Portland's major craft-beer joints, ❺ **BridgePort Brew Pub** (whose winter seasonal brew, Ebenezer Ale, is one of our favorites and whose long-established IPA is a classic example of the style). Though the place has fancied itself up a bit since its no-frills beer-and-pizza early days, hopheads and beer historians will find it well worth a pilgrimage.

Take a right to walk up Northwest Marshall Street, crossing underneath the highway bridges again. This area is loosely known as Slabtown—named for the huge slabs of lumber once used for heat and produced in nearby lumber mills. Turn left on Northwest 16th, and one door over you'll find ❻ **Le Happy,** a sweet little crêperie with a vintage-yellow storefront and a romantic, candlelit interior. Across the street you can see the neon GO BY CAB sign (a riff on Union Station's GO BY TRAIN) marking the old-school brick garage from 1910 that's the headquarters of one of Portland's original taxi companies, Radio Cab, here since 1958.

From Northwest 16th Avenue, take a right on Northwest Lovejoy Street and another right on Northwest 19th Avenue. At Northwest Quimby Street, go left. You'll pass ❼ **Lucky Labrador Beer Hall,** one of several locations for this brewery whose trademark is that people can bring their dogs along while they have a pint. (Note for nontipplers: Lucky Lab also makes its own famously delicious root beer, available in pints or pitchers.)

Continue up Northwest Quimby and take a right on Northwest 21st Avenue. These blocks, most of which were, until recently, enormous parking lots for freight companies, are part of the Conway Master Plan development, which has already started to change the character of this neighborhood pretty substantially and is sure to continue to do so.

Curiosity will draw you into the Freakybuttrue Peculiarium, a museum of oddities.

Turn left on Northwest Thurman Street. In the tall, hot-pink building on your left—you can't miss it—is the ❽ **Freakybuttrue Peculiarium,** a little shop that looks like any old convenience store at first but gets weird once you step inside. A small museum of goofy oddities takes up most of the room; it's silly but fun. (Just don't get your neck stuck in the alien-autopsy display.)

Turn right on Northwest 24th Avenue then right on Northwest Wilson Street. Follow it back to Northwest 22nd Avenue, where you'll turn left to return to the starting point.

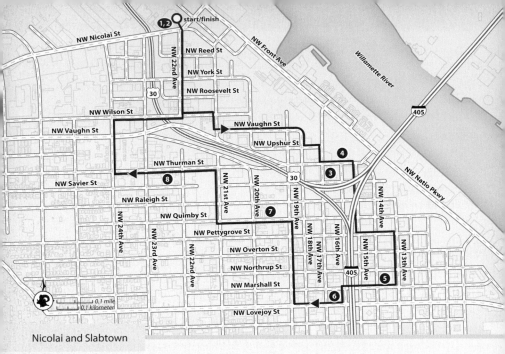

Nicolai and Slabtown

Points of Interest

1. **Ristretto Roasters** ristrettoroasters.com, 2181 NW Nicolai St., 503-227-2866
2. **Schoolhouse Electric & Supply Co.** schoolhouseelectric.com, 2181 NW Nicolai St., 503-230-7113
3. **Olympic Provisions** olympicprovisions.com, 1632 NW Thurman St., 503-894-8136
4. **Breken Kitchen** brekenkitchen.com, 1800 NW 16th Ave., 503-841-6359
5. **BridgePort Brew Pub** bridgeportbrew.com, 1313 NW Marshall St., 503-241-3612
6. **Le Happy** lehappy.com, 1011 NW 16th Ave., 503-226-1258
7. **Lucky Labrador Beer Hall** luckylab.com, 1945 NW Quimby St., 503-517-4352
8. **Freakybuttrue Peculiarium** peculiarium.com, 2234 NW Thurman St.

10 Hawthorne Bridge to Steel Bridge
Ring Around the River

Above: The sternwheeler Portland *houses the Oregon Maritime Museum, great for kids.*

BOUNDARIES: Steel Bridge, SW Front Ave., Hawthorne Bridge, I-5
DISTANCE: 3 miles
DIFFICULTY: Easy
PARKING: Free street parking, metered near Hawthorne side of Eastbank Esplanade
PUBLIC TRANSIT: TriMet Buses 4, 10, and 14 (SW Main St. and Second Ave.); MAX Blue and Red Lines
  (Yamhill District Station)

This is an easy, pleasant (in nice weather) waterfront loop walk that includes two of Portland's more noteworthy, character-defining civic projects, both of which exist mainly thanks to the progressive vision of city leaders who were intent on preserving the city's reputation for pedestrian-friendly travel and that old magazine favorite, livability. Along with great views and fresh air, this walk provides some tangible examples of that often-vague concept, in the form of the Eastbank Esplanade and Waterfront Park. It's also a great way to get a feel for Portland's overall layout, the

Backstory: Dr. James C. Hawthorne

If no one has yet written a historical novel about Hawthorne Boulevard's namesake, it's high time: Dr. James Hawthorne seems like a figure ripe for novelization, at least based on the bare factual outline of his life. A native of Pennsylvania, Hawthorne (1819–1881) spent several years working in medicine in California, where he was also elected to the state Senate. He moved to Portland in 1857 to run a facility for the mentally ill, and then in 1862 he took charge of the Oregon Hospital for the Insane, the state's first such institution (it occupied 200 acres around the intersection of Southeast Hawthorne Boulevard and 10th Avenue). Known as a caring, forward-thinking, and compassionate man, Hawthorne ran the asylum until he died, at which point there were somewhere around 500 inmates. Hawthorne was married twice: his first wife, Emily Curry, died just a few weeks after they were married. In 1865 he married Mrs. E. C. Hite, from Sacramento, and they had three daughters, one of whom died in infancy.

Dr. Hawthorne is buried in Lone Fir Cemetery (see Walk 15: Stark-Belmont); according to the cemetery's website, some 132 of his patients are also buried there, though their graves are unmarked and the exact locations now uncertain. The patients were buried in the same part of the cemetery that was used for Portland's many Chinese workers during the 1890s, some of whom were later disinterred and repatriated for permanent burial in China. Metro, the regional government in charge of Lone Fir maintenance and operation, has planned a memorial garden to commemorate the sad histories of the asylum patients and the Chinese workers who were buried here. (For more about the plan, visit Metro's website, tinyurl.com/lonefirmemorial.)

difference in character between the east side and the west side of the Willamette River, and the importance of bridges and the Willamette River in the city's general atmosphere.

Walk Description

Start at the Salmon Street Springs fountain, at the foot of Southwest Salmon Street near the riverfront. Busy with frolicking toddlers and teens all summer long, the fountain is a familiar and oft-photographed city landmark, as well as a handy meeting point. Fun fact: it has 185 water jets, whose three shifting patterns are controlled by a computer stored underground.

From the fountain, head toward the river and left along the seawall. The original version of this wall was built in the 1920s to keep the Willamette River from flooding downtown every year. What is now Tom McCall Waterfront Park was a major traffic thoroughfare for years, until the opening of the Marquam Bridge and I-5 provided a more efficient alternative. In the late 1960s, then-Governor Tom McCall started looking at plans to replace the outdated road (called Harbor Drive) with some type of public space. (One suggestion, which in retrospect seems borderline insane, was to make Harbor Drive even wider.) The park was finished and dedicated in 1978 and was officially named after McCall in 1984. A tremendously popular place to hang out year-round, it's typically buzzing with a mix of walkers, runners, in-line skaters, napping or lunching office workers, homeless people, tourists, and various festivals. (It's the main location of the annual Rose Festival, for instance, as well as a bunch of summertime music-, beer-, and food-themed extravaganzas.) In 2012 the American Planning Association called it one of the 10 Great Public Spaces, and it's hard to argue with that.

Heading farther north along the waterfront, you'll come to an incongruous white pillar sticking out of the ground. This is the Battleship *Oregon* Memorial, which commemorates a ship from the late 1800s known as the Bulldog of the U.S. Navy; a time capsule in its base is due to be opened in 2076.

Just across the park, at the foot of Southwest Pine Street, is the sternwheeler *Portland*. The ship has been semiretired and is now home to the ❶ **Oregon Maritime Museum**, a kid-friendly favorite among Portland's tourist activities. It usually stays moored but recently has been taken out on occasional summertime exhibition trips. The sternwheeler is the last steam-powered tugboat built and operated in the US; a tour of the ship is included as part of a visit to the Maritime Museum.

Farther along the waterfront, the wide, partly covered plaza that stretches from beneath the Burnside Bridge is the site of Portland's ever-expanding ❷ **Saturday Market**, a weekly outdoor arts and crafts and food bonanza that involves a satisfying amount of street theater and, naturally, sugarcoated elephant-ear pastries alongside tie-dyed clogs and vegan dream catchers. It runs every weekend (including Sundays, despite the name) from March until Christmas Eve.

On the other side of the Burnside Bridge, at the foot of Northwest Couch Street, is the Japanese American Historical Plaza. During World War II, Japanese Americans in the area were forced into internment camps; this plaza is dedicated to their memories, and artwork in the memorial garden portrays important moments from Japanese-American history.

Continue along the waterfront path until you come to the Steel Bridge. Take the stairs up to the upper level (you can also stay on the lower level and cross that way; it's equally interesting either way, but the views are just slightly better from the top level). Opened in 1912, the Steel Bridge was built for the Union Pacific Railroad, and in choosing which level to take you've already discovered one of its unique characteristics: it has two decks that can move independently. The lower deck is designed for walkers, cyclists, and railroad traffic, while the upper level is for motorized traffic and light rail.

At the far (east) end of the bridge, zigzag your way right, to ground level, to link with the Eastbank Esplanade.

Eastbank Esplanade, Portland's *other* long-and-skinny riverside greenway, is perhaps best loved for the views it provides of Tom McCall Waterfront Park. Which isn't to say it lacks its own charms. But its proximity to highways and the constraints of geography—it fits rather snugly into the thin space that has been allotted for it—mean there isn't much greenery to pretty up the path. It's kind of utilitarian, which doesn't bother the joggers and cyclists who use it one bit. Besides, the views across the river are glorious, and the esplanade is attractive in its own *Gattaca*-esque way. The walkway was dedicated to former Mayor Vera Katz (who fought for the park and is primarily responsible for its construction) in 2004. It's 1.5 miles long, extending from the Steel Bridge to the Hawthorne Bridge. The walkway is illuminated at night, which is particularly great during winter when it gets dark early (and light late). A 1,200-foot section floats out over the water, lending the esplanade a romantic, marina-like feel. It's also an environmental asset: part of the trail doubles as a water-treatment system, filtering runoff from I-5 before it gets to the river. Public art installations are found at several points along the trail—beneath the Morrison Bridge, look for *Echo Gate,* a copper sculpture meant to mirror downtown Portland's historic architecture. Another favorite is *Ghost Ship,* an impressive work in glass, copper, and steel.

Follow the esplanade all the way to its end at the Hawthorne Bridge, winding your way up the circular path onto the bridge. The Hawthorne is the only vertical-lift bridge in North America that's older than the Steel Bridge. If you commute with any frequency between downtown and Southeast Portland, you may be convinced that the bridge is perpetually being raised, and in fact it does lift around 200 times a month. Aside from making way for tall river traffic, the bridge needs to move at least once every 8 hours in order to keep its gears from sticking. (Don't worry—if you're walking across, you'll have plenty of warning before it goes up.) As you walk across the seams in the panels that form the pedestrian walkway, look down for a little dose of vertigo.

As you come to the end of the bridge, turn right and descend the stairs to rejoin the Waterfront Park path and return to your starting point.

Connecting the Walks

Link with **Walk 1: Old Town and Chinatown** (page 4), **Walk 12: Industrial Southeast** (page 59), or **Walk 14: Hawthorne Boulevard** (page 72) from various points along this route.

Hawthorne Bridge to Steel Bridge

Points of Interest

1 Oregon Maritime Museum oregonmaritimemuseum.org, 115 SW Ash St., 503-224-7724

2 Saturday Market portlandsaturdaymarket.com, 2 SW Naito Pkwy.

View of Tom McCall Waterfront Park from the Eastbank Esplanade

11 Tram to South Waterfront
The Sci-fi Walk

Above: The aerial tram carries passengers from OHSU to the South Waterfront neighborhood.

BOUNDARIES: Willamette River, SW Gibbs St., SW Abernethy St., SW 10th Ave.
DISTANCE: 2 miles
DIFFICULTY: Easy (or moderate if you add a Marquam Trail hike)
PARKING: Metered, in OHSU lot
PUBLIC TRANSIT: TriMet Bus 8 (OHSU), tram, Portland Streetcar to downtown

If you, too, grew up devouring unhealthy quantities of science-fiction paperbacks with garishly painted covers, you will automatically love the Portland Aerial Tram. Who cares if it's practical? *Look at it!* The tram makes Portland's skyline 50 times more awesome than before. Its other purpose, of course, is to carry people between Oregon Health & Science University (OHSU), perched high on the hillside, and the South Waterfront, a newly developed neighborhood in a previously industrial area alongside the river south of downtown. The South Waterfront development occupies a former brownfield—land that was contaminated with the by-products of heavy industrial use, and which required a $20 million cleanup effort that has been going on since the 1990s. (A large portion of the industry that once occupied this area involved barge building, which continued until as recently as 2017, when the mammoth Zidell company launched its last barge. Before that, U.S. Navy ships were built here for World War II and then dismantled here afterward.) The cleanup of the area is essentially finished, and development continues—the location of this neighborhood makes it a potentially very exciting area for developers.

This walk takes us via the tram from OHSU's Marquam Hill location down through the South Waterfront neighborhood, with a bit of exploring on top of the hill first for those who are so inclined. If you're feeling even more ambitious, Metro (the regional government) maintains a linked network called the 4T Trail: it forms a loop that incorporates the Portland Streetcar, which connects to MAX light rail, which leads to the Wildwood Trail, which takes you to the tram (trail, tram, trolley, train = four Ts). Maps and guides are available online at library.oregonmetro.gov /files/trailtramtrolleytrain.pdf.

Note: Due to space constraints, our map begins at the south PAT terminal and does not show the upper PAT terminal or Marquam Nature Park. You can find maps of the park online at fmnp. org or at the Marquam Shelter, at the Marquam Trail entrance.

Walk Description

Start at the upper terminal of the Portland Aerial Tram, in the OHSU Hospital complex. While you're up here, take advantage of the easy access to the wilderness trails through ❶ **Marquam Nature Park,** a 176-acre wilderness laced with around 5 miles of trails. To reach the closest trail-head, turn left along Southwest Sam Jackson Park Road, past several OHSU buildings; then turn right on Southwest Ninth Avenue and, tucked behind the motorcycle and scooter parking, you'll see the sign marking the start of Connor Trail. This path loops around toward the west and south to eventually meet up with the Marquam Trail, part of the regional 40-Mile Loop system (see Backstory: 40-Mile Loop, page 56), and is well worth a detour if you have the time.

Retrace your steps back along Southwest Sam Jackson Park Road to reach the upper terminal of the Aerial Tram. Riding the tram costs $4.90 round-trip (unless you have a TriMet monthly or annual pass or a Portland streetcar annual pass already), takes 4 minutes one-way, and runs about every 6 minutes most days. Aside from being adorable, the tram was also an audacious under-taking design-wise, and rather expensive. As with most such ambitious projects, its construction was not without detractors. Some neighbors (bafflingly) felt that the tram would not aesthetically enhance the Portland skyline. Most of the criticism, though, was budgetary—especially

Backstory: 40-Mile Loop

If you spend any time at all hiking, cycling, or planning routes on trails in the Portland area, you're likely to hear about the 40-Mile Loop metro-area trail system. This, as you might imagine, is a system of interconnected trails, some well established and others still in the planning stages. It includes the excellent Wildwood Trail through Forest Park, as well as bike-friendly urban corridors like the I-205 Path, Springwater Corridor, and Eastbank Esplanade. The "40-Mile" part of the name refers to city leaders' original conception of a regional trail network, an idea first dreamed up a century ago; when trail advocates revived the project in 1982, they called it the 40-Mile Loop in honor of that original vision.

These days the trail plan covers several cities and counties close to Portland, and the total mileage of the envisioned trail network is more like 950; the Multnomah County section alone incorporates some 30 parks and 140 miles of trail. For more details about the 40-Mile Loop, including maps of current and future trails, visit 40mileloop.org (you can also get maps and information at Portland visitor centers).

after the projected cost of the tram doubled during the planning process. Some residents wondered if it was fair for taxpayers to foot part of the bill for a service that would be used primarily by OHSU students and staff. (The city's share of the total cost was 15%, or $8.5 million.) Ultimately, though, the project was approved, and the tram opened to the public in December 2006. It has carried more than 5 million riders so far. Its construction paved the way for development in the South Waterfront area, particularly by OHSU.

The lower (southern) terminal of the tram is at OHSU's lower office building, near the north side of the South Waterfront development. (Adding to the whole cuteness factor, the lower lawn is "mowed" each year by three or four goats. *Aww.*) The popular ❷ **Daily Cafe**, inside the lower tram terminal, is a good option for refreshments in this neighborhood (and used to be one of the few options here, period, but happily there are a lot more choices than there were in the neighborhood's early days, mostly along Southwest Moody Avenue). Take Southwest Bond Avenue a block south to Elizabeth Caruthers Park, where among other things there's a weekly farmers market (Thursday afternoons, June–October). Cross the park diagonally to the corner of Southwest Moody Avenue and Gaines Street. Take a left at Gaines Street.

Where Gaines meets Southwest Bond Avenue, you'll come to one of the earliest dining options to be established in this neighborhood: ❸ **Bambuza Vietnam Bistro.** (All the neighborhood's new buildings are designed with retail and dining on the ground level, and the spaces have gradually filled up.) Across the street is an outpost of ❹ **Little Big Burger,** a more casual choice for a quick bite. You're basically in the heart of the development now; even a few years on, it's still new enough and shiny enough to have a distinctly futuristic feel.

Follow Southwest Bond Avenue north for a block, then turn right (east) at Southwest Pennoyer Street. At River Parkway, turn right, then left on Southwest Gaines Street, which leads to a short pedestrian-only path along the riverfront. Follow the path to its end, take in the view across the water—you can see the Ross Island Bridge, as well as Ross Island itself, where if you're lucky (or carry binoculars) you might spot one of the bald eagles that live and nest on the island—then retrace your steps to the intersection of River Parkway and Gaines.

Continue straight (west) on Gaines, then take your first right on Southwest Bond Avenue, where you can hop back on the tram or catch a streetcar toward downtown.

Shiny new apartment buildings in the heart of South Waterfront

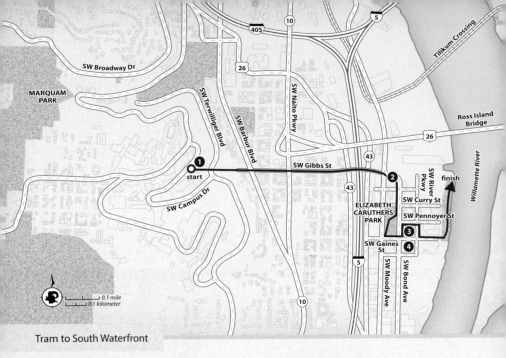

Tram to South Waterfront

Points of Interest

1. **Marquam Nature Park** fmnp.org, SW Sam Jackson Park Rd. and SW Marquam St.
2. **Daily Cafe at the Tram** dailycafe.net, 3355 SW Bond Ave., 503-224-9691
3. **Bambuza Vietnam Bistro** bambuza.com, 3682 SW Bond Ave., 503-206-6330
4. **Little Big Burger** littlebigburger.com, 3704 SW Bond Ave., 503-265-8021

12   Industrial Southeast
Produce Row

Above: Canard café and cocktail bar

BOUNDARIES: NE Couch St., SE 11th Ave., Willamette River, SE Division St.
DISTANCE: 2.5 miles
DIFFICULTY: Easy
PARKING: Free street parking, $3 in lot at OMSI
PUBLIC TRANSIT: TriMet Buses 4, 6, 10, and 14 at Hawthorne Bridge; Buses 12, 19, and 20
    at E. Burnside St. and NE Sandy Blvd.

An amorphous area sometimes called the Eastside Industrial or Southeast Warehouse District, sometimes Produce Row, this part of town is currently among the fastest-changing. At its northwest corner, two enormous and striking new buildings—the Yard and the Dumbbell—have radically altered the city's skyline and the general mood of the surrounding streets, and there are sure to be more where those came from. But tucked away just below these gleaming cubes is the world-famous Burnside Skate Park, which remains as undeniable evidence of the area's cool, scrappy, rough-around-the-edges vibe. Industrial Southeast can still legitimately be described as gritty (and I mean that in a good way). This is partly by design: the Central Eastside Industrial Council, a nonprofit group that looks out for the neighborhood's business interests, continues to lobby to keep housing out of the area to preserve its cool working-class feel (and prevent it from turning into the Pearl District). But it's not all rail yards and storage units here. A number of distilleries have set up shop in the neighborhood, creating a Distillery Row that offers drop-in tastings at several venues on weekends. (See distilleryrowpdx.com for details about the various venues and how to get a tasting-room "passport.") One neighborhood landmark, the Produce Row Café, was snazzed up a few years ago with a total remodel, and several other chic new dining and drinking establishments have helped amp up the sophistication level, ready or not.

Walk Description

Start at the bus stop at Northeast Couch Street and 12th Avenue. Movie nerds should pause and take a look down Northeast 12th Avenue to the right, where you'll spot a yellow-and-blue house you might recognize from director Kelly Reichardt's 2006 movie *Old Joy*. And beyond that you'll see a well-loved Portland icon: the gigantic rotating loaf of bread that designates Franz Bakery, whose intoxicating aroma you can also usually smell from here depending on the time of day.

Turn left and head down Northeast 12th Avenue, then cross East Burnside Street and turn right. (This intersection is notoriously confusing and can be a little hairy—stay alert.) On the left is ❶ **Hippo Hardware,** an oddball hardware store and local landmark whose labyrinthine interior is a gold mine of old rusty hinges, Victorian doorknobs, weird lamps, skeleton keys, and all sorts of antique fixtures. Treasure hunt!

Two blocks down on the left are the ❷ **Jupiter Hotel** and ❸ **Doug Fir Lounge,** formerly the Chinese Tea House—which had a brief but crucial career as an indie-rock venue—and now a boutique hotel with an attached 300-capacity live-music venue, bar, and restaurant whose design set (or at least embraced) all kinds of trends when it opened in 2004. The Doug Fir's upstairs restaurant-bar is what you might imagine every building in Aspen or Vail will look like in the future: rustic but glittery, simultaneously posh and woodsy. The restrooms are paneled in gold-veined mirror—totally disorienting, but kind of fabulous. Downstairs, the music venue leans more toward the log-cabin feel, and regardless of your feelings about the Doug Fir as a whole, it's a great place to see bands you love: everyone sounds fantastic here. The attached Jupiter Hotel works a sort of *Jetsons*–IKEA minimalist design into a 1960s motor-inn shape, and the small art gallery in its front office has interesting exhibits that change monthly. Just across Southeast

Ninth Avenue from the Jupiter is its big-sister hotel, ❹ **Jupiter NEXT,** a 67-room boutique hotel in a design-heavy, asymmetrical building. If the original Jupiter has finally achieved a worn-in feel, the new digs still sparkle. The lobby bar, Hey Love, has a roster of kitchen and bar staff with long histories in some top Portland drinking establishments (Dig a Pony, Rum Club).

Across the street, and again in the next block, you'll find several funky little vintage-clothing shops, novelty shops, and galleries well worth poking around in.

In the next block you'll find one of the most talked-about restaurants in a much-talked-about restaurant scene: the always-packed ❺ **Le Pigeon,** run by James Beard Award–winning chef Gabriel Rucker. It's a beautiful, smallish space with an open kitchen and a meat-heavy dinner menu. Its sister spot, the café-cocktail bar ❻ **Canard,** has just opened next door and is well worth a stop too. It has a more casual, wine-bar feel and a great happy hour; try one of the little steam burgers, or the enormous brunch dish that's basically a towering stack of pancakes smothered in duck gravy and topped with seared foie gras and a duck egg. Nobody lives forever.

Hunt for treasure at Hippo Hardware.

Continue down Burnside past a string of appealingly rock 'n' roll bars to Northeast Sixth Avenue. Turn right on Sixth, then left on Northeast Couch Street. At the corner of Couch and Northeast Grand Avenue. you'll find ❼ **Stark's Vacuum Museum,** a strange little space inside a retail vacuum-cleaner store, where some 300 models of vacuums from various points in history (starting in the 1800s) are stored. It's free to go in, have a look, and count your blessings.

Go one block farther along Northeast Couch, then turn left onto Northeast Martin Luther King Jr. Boulevard for a block. Cross the street and turn right to walk along East Burnside Street, just underneath the bridge ramp. Here, tucked under the east end of the bridge, is the ❽ **Burnside Skatepark,** one of the first and generally considered one of the best skate parks in the country and—even if you're not into skating—an inspiring community project.

Before about 1990, underneath the Burnside Bridge was not a place you'd ever want to go. But a handful of skater kids started reclaiming the area, gradually adding to the empty concrete square until it became the enclosed park it is now. This took more than a decade, and the feat of the park's construction is amazing in itself, but the real victory is that Burnside Skatepark, though built without permission, eventually won tentative acceptance by city government as a public skate park.

Right next to the park, with a design that echoes many of its features, is the new location of ❾ **Tilt,** a bar and burger restaurant known for yet another enormous sandwich, the Big Tilt Burger. (It's huge.) The industrial-chic interior is built around a massive concrete tube-shaped frame, inside of which stretches the long, narrow bar; in the rest of the space, utilitarian details are almost too cute—think red shop towels instead of napkins, outdoor decking material used for seating, light fixtures made out of repurposed metal strips that any plumber or construction worker will recognize. It's the kind of place you almost hate to admit actually looks pretty cool. What you don't want to do here is fall down: the place is all sharp corners and unforgiving surfaces, so drink cautiously and watch your footing. You might consider embracing the skate-park theme and wear a helmet.

Tilt occupies the lower level of the Yard, a love it or hate it (but definitely can't ignore it) 21-story apartment building that has lurked menacingly over the east side of the Burnside Bridge since 2016. The building's design creates the impression that the crew of an Imperial Star Destroyer just decided to park on the bridge for a sec while they popped in to grab a coffee down the street. It's a little scary. Cheering things up significantly is the nearby (and even more conspicuous) office building known as the Fair-Haired Dumbbell. You can't miss it: a bright, colorful mural by artist James Jean covers every inch of the building's exterior. For better or worse, this is not your father's Portland skyline.

Retrace your steps up East Burnside Street and take a right on Southeast Third Avenue, then a left on Southeast Ankeny Street, then a right onto Southeast Martin Luther King Jr. Boulevard. At the corner of MLK and Southeast Oak Street you'll find the ❿ **Sheridan Fruit Company,** a small grocery store that has been owned and operated by the same family since 1946. The produce and the deli here are excellent.

Follow Southeast Oak Street two blocks west to Southeast Second Avenue, where you'll come to the neighborhood's longstanding namesake pub, ⓫ **Produce Row Café.** This former workingman's beer bar and sandwich shop has undergone a radical transformation since its early days. It was always comfy, but now it's also stylish, and the back patio has been covered to accommodate the long rainy season. Food options at the old ProRow consisted of a few types of legendarily enormous sandwiches; these days you can get $9 avocado toast and a quinoa bowl, too. One thing that hasn't changed, thank goodness, is the massive beer selection (now with whiskey!).

From Southeast Oak Street, turn left onto Southeast Second Avenue to reach the imposing, mustard-yellow ⑫ **Olympic Mills Commerce Center,** one of the more attractive structures in the area. Renovated and retrofitted in 2008, this large, open-format industrial space was originally the Olympic Cereal Mill, built in 1920. During the 1920s it was home to a General Mills subsidiary that churned out boxes of Wheaties. Today its tenants include, among other things, the highbrow charcuterie joint Olympia Provisions, which is about as far from a box of cereal as it's possible to get.

Continue along Southeast Second Avenue and turn left at Southeast Morrison Street. At the corner of Morrison and Southeast Third Avenue is ⑬ **Le Bistro Montage,** whose mere name elicits gazes of dreamy nostalgia in Portland scenesters of a certain age. It was the ultimate late-night postclub dining spot during the 1990s (it opened in 1992 and was named Restaurant of the Year that year by local alt-weekly *Willamette Week*). It was, and still is, open for dinner until 4 a.m. Fridays and Saturdays, catering largely to the wasted and famished. Things that made it brilliant include white-clothed communal tables, "pounder" bottles of Rainier, frog legs, extremely cheap mac-and-cheese with odd enhancements (such as Spam, alligator, or crushed Oreos), oyster shooters (if you asked for one, the waiters would bellow your order to the kitchen at the tops of their lungs), *The Last Supper* and other humongous paintings on the walls, red wine in little jelly jars, and the swan and other animal-shaped tinfoil packages your leftovers would be wrapped in. (Most of that is still true, but fashions change; Montage no longer seems to be the place where *everyone* must appear after the bars close.)

Turn right on Southeast Third Avenue, then right again on Southeast Belmont Street to walk on the cobbled streets underneath the bridge ramp, between the columns. This part of town seems built for a Hollywood car chase. At Southeast Water Avenue turn left to pass the ⑭ **Hair of the Dog Brewing Company,** home of one of Portland's first and still most highly regarded microbrewers. Stop in for a taste or a tour. Just ahead you'll see the Eastbank Commerce Center, another attractive and newish, or at least newly renovated, warehouse building. Across the street, its sibling, the Water Avenue Commerce Center, is home to the excellent ⑮ **Water Avenue Coffee.** (The small roastery-café's alluring blue neon COFFEE sign beckons the undercaffeinated at all hours; the coffee can also be found in several Portland cafés and restaurants.) In the same building, Bunk Bar has awesome sandwiches and occasional live music.

Turn left on Southeast Taylor Street, then take a right on Southeast Second Avenue.

Follow Southeast Second through a few industrial blocks; at Southeast Clay Street, take a right. When you get back to Southeast Water Avenue, turn left and follow Water to the parking lot of the ⑯ **Oregon Museum of Science and Industry** (OMSI).

OMSI sits perched over the river at the southern end of the Eastside Industrial district. It's a great resource for anyone with kids, partly because, like a good Pixar movie, it's also fun for adults. The building, transformed from an old power plant, opened in 1992, but parts of the collection are much older, having belonged to the Portland Free Museum before being moved to OMSI at its old location near the zoo. These days, the museum hosts a number of permanent and rotating exhibitions, most of them with hands-on elements and all of them educational in a nonintimidating, science-is-fun kind of way (a regular installation on snot is a big early-winter draw). There's also a planetarium, an IMAX theater, and the submarine from *The Hunt for Red October*.

To get back to your starting point, retrace your steps to Southeast Hawthorne Boulevard, turn right, and catch MAX light rail at Southeast Grand Avenue. Get off at East Burnside Street and walk back up to Northeast 12th Avenue.

Connecting the Walks

This walk links easily with **Walk 10: Hawthorne Bridge to Steel Bridge** (page 49), as well as with **Walk 14: Hawthorne Boulevard** (page 72).

Shops on East Burnside Street

Industrial Southeast

Points of Interest

1. Hippo Hardware hippohardware.com, 1040 E. Burnside St., 503-231-1444
2. Jupiter Hotel jupiterhotel.com, 800 E. Burnside St., 503-230-9200
3. Doug Fir Lounge dougfirlounge.com, 830 E. Burnside St., 503-231-9663
4. Jupiter NEXT jupiterhotel.com, 900 E. Burnside St., 503-230-9200
5. Le Pigeon lepigeon.com, 738 E. Burnside St., 503-546-8796
6. Canard canardpdx.com, 734 E. Burnside St., 971-279-2356
7. Stark's Vacuum Museum starks.com/vacuum-museum, 107 NE Grand Ave., 800-230-4101
8. Burnside Skatepark East side of Burnside Bridge
9. Tilt tiltitup.com, 22 NE Second Ave., 971-420-2165
10. Sheridan Fruit Company sheridanfruit.com, 409 SE Martin Luther King Jr. Blvd., 503-236-2114
11. Produce Row Café producerowcafe.com, 204 SE Oak St., 503-232-8355
12. Olympic Mills Commerce Center 107 SE Washington St.
13. Le Bistro Montage montageportland.com, 301 SE Morrison St., 503-234-1324
14. Hair of the Dog Brewing Company hairofthedog.com, 61 SE Water Ave., 503-232-6585
15. Water Avenue Coffee wateravenuecoffee.com, 1028 SE Water Ave., 503-808-7083
16. Oregon Museum of Science and Industry omsi.edu, 1945 SE Water Ave., 503-797-4640

13 Division/Clinton, Ladd's Addition
Theater of the Street

Above: Clinton Street Pub is a friendly, old-school dive next door to the Clinton Street Theater.

BOUNDARIES: SE 12th Ave., SE Hawthorne Blvd., SE 39th Ave., SE Clinton St.
DISTANCE: About 3.25 miles
DIFFICULTY: Easy
PARKING: Free street parking
PUBLIC TRANSIT: TriMet Bus 10 (SE Clinton St. and 26th Ave.) or Bus 4 (SE Division and 37th Ave.)

A little pocket of Southeast Portland cool, the Division/Clinton area has been steadily gaining ground in recent years as a food-and-nightlife destination and these days is wildly popular with locals and visitors alike. It might be the part of Portland that's changed the most in the years since the first edition of this book. In fact, this is a good place to issue the caveat that any bar or restaurant mentioned here is very likely to have become something else by the time you read this. Division Street in particular is changing quickly and constantly, and it's fascinating but a little scary to watch. Slick new apartment buildings line the street alongside dozens of brand-new, top-10-must-visit bars and restaurants, in what just a few years ago was a cheap, mostly residential, totally unglamorous neighborhood. Increased urban density is a good thing—don't get me wrong. And the buzzing street life here is fantastic, as long as you're on foot. But one result of all the new development is that already too-narrow Division Street has become a pedestrian-dodging gauntlet for drivers, and on-street parking is such a hot commodity that local residents have lodged complaints against new apartment buildings being designed without parking spaces. (Short version: don't try to drive; take the bus here.)

Ultimately, of course, so much development and new business is good news for this area—if nothing else, it makes for a diverting walk with plenty of inviting places to linger and refuel. This walk also includes one of the city's prettiest residential areas, the labyrinthine Ladd's Addition, a small, historic neighborhood whose skewed angle and repeating pattern of diamond-shaped rose gardens make it almost as disorienting as it is attractive.

Walk Description

Start at one of the early anchors of the tiny Clinton neighborhood, the ❶ Clinton Street Theater. Though it has changed hands frequently over the years, the Clinton has maintained a fairly consistent aesthetic sensibility, one that embraces the fringe of independent cinema. And I don't mean *fringe* and *independent* as in Sundance; I mean everything from Japanese gore-horror to local filmed-by-bike shorts to low-budget music documentaries. The theater's claim to fame, however—and its sustaining force—is *The Rocky Horror Picture Show,* which the Clinton has screened at midnight every Saturday since time began, more or less. If you've never seen *Rocky Horror,* it's worth investigating, if only for the vivid characters waiting in line to buy tickets. Next door to the theater is another of Portland's increasingly rare old-school dive bars, the Clinton Street Pub, a no-frills joint with pinball and cheap drinks.

Across the street are two other great Portland institutions: ❷ Dots Cafe, a dimly lit, red-brocade-wallpapered restaurant and bar decorated with velvet matador paintings (it recently changed ownership but seems to be going strong and largely unchanged), and ❸ Clinton Street Video, one of the last independent video stores in town (or anywhere, for that matter). It's owned by Chris Slusarenko, whose decades-deep roots in the local music scene—he fronted Sub Pop Records band Sprinkler in the early 1990s and played bass with Guided By Voices—may help explain the store's killer inventory of all things music-related.

From the video store, turn right to head west along Southeast Clinton Street. At Southeast 21st Avenue, you'll reach a little hub of lively bars and restaurants that have all cropped up in the past few years. A good choice for both food and drinks is the ❹ **Night Light Lounge,** one of the groundbreakers on this corner, with its romantic lighting, comfy couches in the back room, and mostly enclosed outdoor seating on the patio.

Continue down Southeast Clinton Street to Southeast 13th Avenue and turn right. At Southeast Ivon Street go left, then turn right on Southeast 12th Avenue. At the end of the block on your right you'll come to the delightful eat–drink combo that is ❺ **Los Gorditos** taqueria and ❻ **Apex** bar. Round the corner to the right at Southeast Division Street, then go on in and refresh yourself. The taqueria started as a popular food cart, still in its original location farther up Division, at Southeast 50th Avenue. As for Apex, it has so many beers on tap that its computerized beer menu looks like the arrivals-and-departures board at an airport; it doesn't serve food, but you're allowed and encouraged to bring in edibles from Los Gorditos next door.

If you're more of a cocktail person than a beer nerd, walk west along Division Street, crossing 10th Avenue, and look for the stunning mural (by the artist Fin Dac) on the wall of a building at Southeast Ninth Avenue and Division (note her cool hairdo of living plants). Inside is a delightful, summery cocktail bar called ❼ **Palomar,** recommended for fancy daiquiris and Cuban dishes.

Once sated, turn and continue walking back east up Southeast Division Street. Hang a left at Southeast 16th Avenue to wander into the Ladd's Addition area. Notice on the right the ❽ **St. Philip Neri Catholic Church** complex, part of which was designed by architect Pietro Belluschi, whose fingerprints, you'll come to discover, are all over the city. (The original church was built by Joseph Jacobberger in 1913; Belluschi's addition is from 1949.)

In two blocks you'll reach the first of the funky, slightly askew green spaces that make Ladd's Addition both wonderful and deeply confusing. It's easy to lose your way in this tangled nest of streets, but on the other hand, this is kind of a nice place in which to be lost. Ladd's Addition is Portland's oldest planned residential neighborhood; it has been a designated historic district with the National Register of Historic Places since 1988. It's roughly pinwheel-shaped, with four diamond-shaped green spaces and a central park area that all hold rose test gardens, and tree-lined residential streets in between, with homes built primarily from 1905 to 1930. The neighborhood is named after William Ladd, a merchant and mid-19th-century Portland mayor whose farm was here. (See Backstory: William S. Ladd, opposite page.)

When you get to the first of the diamond-shaped green spaces, walk around it on the right-hand side and continue north along Southeast 16th Avenue. You'll soon reach Ladd's Circle, the main parklike hub. Turn right here; pass Southeast Ladd Avenue, and note ❾ **Palio Dessert & Espresso House** on the right. One of the very few businesses within Ladd's Addition, Palio is open until 11 p.m., unusual for a coffee shop in Portland; the back room is lined with books, adding to

Backstory: William S. Ladd

It's not easy to imagine what Portland must've looked like when 24-year-old William Ladd arrived, in 1851, from New Hampshire with a shipment of booze to sell. But Ladd's impact on the way the city looks today is clear: he's at least partly responsible for some of its most beautiful areas, including Laurelhurst Park, Ladd's Addition, and the Crystal Springs Rhododendron Garden.

When Ladd made his way here, it was two years after gold had been found in California, and Portland was not much more than a rest area on the way to San Francisco, or a place where those who'd struck out could pause and lick their wounds. A census from around that time—December 1850—put the city's population at 821.

Ladd quickly made a name for himself. He set up shop immediately selling the liquor he'd brought, but within just a few days he had expanded his range of goods. Apparently he knew what he was doing. By 1853 he was able to build a storefront on Front Avenue, the first one made of brick in Portland. Teaming up with other investors, in the next several years he started railroad, shipping, manufacturing, and telegraph companies, not to mention the public library and River View Cemetery. With his original East Coast business partner, he founded the Ladd and Tilton Bank, Portland's first, in 1859. Ladd served as Portland's mayor from 1854 to 1855. He remained a well-regarded civic leader and businessman until he died.

Ladd was buried in River View Cemetery on January 9, 1893. In a bizarre coda, a few years later a care-taker found that his grave had been dug up and the body was missing. Ladd's remains, which had been taken for ransom, were eventually tracked down to the west side of the Willamette River, along what is now Macadam Avenue, and the thieves were arrested. He was reburied at River View—this time in cement.

the quiet, library-esque atmosphere of the place. Turn right on Southeast Harrison Street, then right again on Southeast Cypress Street; then take two quick lefts to circumnavigate the rose-garden patch. You'll end up on Southeast Locust Avenue; turn right here, walk two blocks, then go left on Southeast Hazel Street. Follow Hazel until it becomes the Holly Street–16th Avenue Alley.

The alleys in Ladd's Addition were initially planned as back-door service roads for the upper-crust homes envisioned here. (You'll walk right behind one such home between Southeast Poplar Street and 16th Avenue; it has the block to itself.) Today the alleys are considered public rights-of-way, open to foot and vehicle traffic, but most are unmaintained.

Cross Southeast 16th Avenue and stay in the alley for another block; cross Southeast Maple Street to continue on Southeast Palm Street. Turn left at Southeast Ladd Avenue. On your left, in an unassuming bungalow, is the quirky ❿ **Hat Museum** (open by appointment only, $35 admission). Inside the 1910 Craftsman-style Ladd-Reingold House is a collection of not just hats but all sorts of random-seeming miscellany. Be prepared for eccentricity (and mermaids).

Walk across Ladd's Circle and continue along elm-lined Southeast Ladd Avenue. When you reach the three-way intersection of Ladd Avenue, Southeast 20th Avenue, and Southeast Division Street, turn left to walk up Division.

On the left, at Southeast Division and Southeast 25th Avenue (across from the legitimately divey Reel M Inn bar), you'll see ⓫ **Langlitz Leathers,** one of Portland's coolest home-grown businesses. Ross Langlitz started it in 1947 after making his own protective gear for his motorcycle-racing habit (he was a devoted rider all his life, despite having lost a leg in a motorcycle accident at age 17). Langlitz jackets these days are internationally sought-after, but it's still a family business (Ross's granddaughter runs it now). Pop in and check out Ross's beloved Velocette hanging from the ceiling.

Continue walking up Southeast Division Street, through increasing numbers of new housing and businesses, mostly bars and restaurants. This neighborhood has been transformed in recent years; it's officially a destination now, and one of the big draws is celebrated chef Andy Ricker's Thai restaurant ⓬ **Pok Pok,** which has built an empire on a pile of chicken wings. Pok Pok started as a rickety little takeout shack in front of Ricker's house, with a brief menu inspired by some of the culinary revelations he had encountered as a young backpacker in the 1980s and then spent decades researching. The place quickly became so popular he had to expand it into the rest of the house, and he later opened several other locations in Portland and elsewhere. You'll see Pok Pok on your right as you cross Southeast 32nd Avenue. Diagonally across Division Street is its companion bar, the Whiskey Soda Lounge, which Ricker conceived as a place for "the drinking foods of Thailand"; it serves as a comfortable place to wait for a table at the restaurant. (You can get many of the Pok Pok dishes here too.)

At the corner of Southeast Division Street and 37th Avenue is the ⓭ **Victory Bar,** a nice stopping point, with an ace menu of comfort food (hush puppies, baked spaetzle) and bartenders with stellar cocktail-mixing pedigrees.

From here you can take TriMet Bus 4 back down to Southeast Division and 26th Avenue, then walk two blocks south to return to the starting point.

Division/Clinton, Ladd's Addition

Points of Interest

1. **Clinton Street Theater** cstpdx.com, 2522 SE Clinton St., 503-238-5588

2. **Dots Cafe** dotscafeportland.com, 2521 SE Clinton St., 503-235-0203

3. **Clinton Street Video** 2501 SE Clinton St., 503-236-9030

4. **Night Light Lounge** nightlightlounge.net, 2100 SE Clinton St., 503-731-6500

5. **Los Gorditos** losgorditospdx.com, 1212 SE Division St., 503-445-6289

6. **Apex** apexbar.com, 1216 SE Division St., 503-273-9227

7. **Palomar** barpalomar.com, 959 SE Division St., 971-266-8276

8. **St. Philip Neri Catholic Church** stphilipneripdx.org, 2408 SE 16th Ave., 503-231-4955

9. **Palio Dessert & Espresso House** palio-in-ladds.com, 1996 SE Ladd Ave., 503-232-9412

10. **The Hat Museum** thehatmuseum.com, 1928 SE Ladd Ave., 503-232-0433

11. **Langlitz Leathers** langlitz.com, 2443 SE Division St., 503-235-0959

12. **Pok Pok** pokpokpdx.com, 3226 SE Division St., 503-232-1387

13. **Victory Bar** thevictorybar.com, 3652 SE Division St., 503-236-8755

14 Hawthorne Boulevard
Tabor to the River

Above: The Back Stage Bar at Bagdad Theater & Pub, part of the local McMenamins chain

BOUNDARIES: SE Hawthorne Blvd., SE 60th Ave., Willamette River
DISTANCE: 3.5 miles
DIFFICULTY: Easy (moderate if done in reverse)
PARKING: Free street parking
PUBLIC TRANSIT: TriMet Bus 71 (SE 60th Ave. and Hawthorne) and Bus 14 (all along Hawthorne)

When Portlanders talk about Hawthorne, as in the district, they're usually thinking of a fairly small section of this major Southeast thoroughfare, from about 30th to 39th Avenues (although in fact the walk-friendly portion of the street extends for most of its length, as you'll discover). These few blocks used to require stepping gingerly over reclining neo-hippies and their pets, feeling your way through clouds of patchouli and coming to terms with the idea of Caucasian dreadlocks. There were bead shops, burnouts, and the occasional didgeridoo. These days, as Southeast

Portland has continued to gentrify, the vibe along Hawthorne has shifted slightly away from full-on hippie, and the district feels a little more mainstream, for better or worse.

Perhaps fittingly, the street and district are named for the founder of Oregon's first mental hospital (see Backstory: Dr. James C. Hawthorne on page 50); Hawthorne Boulevard was once called Asylum Street. The street bisects Southeast Portland in all its multilayered glory, from the volcano to the river, from artistry to industry. (For more of a workout, try the route in reverse—it's on a slight but noticeable incline, and you can scamper to the top of Mount Tabor if you haven't had enough by the time you reach the end.)

Walk Description

Start at the stairs leading from Southeast 60th Avenue up the hill to Reservoir #6 on Mount Tabor. If you're feeling sprightly, hop up the staircase for a view across town; if you're really energetic, take the *next* set of stairs as well for an even better view from a reservoir one level higher. Mount Tabor is a dormant volcano, and the park that occupies it is one of the jewels of the city; it's a fantastic and very easily accessible bit of wilderness in which to stroll around, have a picnic, walk the dog, or get a workout. And the views from its higher reaches are spectacular in several directions. (Mount Tabor is also the location of the annual Portland Adult Soapbox Derby—see Backstory on page 75.)

Once back on Southeast 60th Avenue, hang a right to reach Southeast Hawthorne Boulevard, then turn left down Hawthorne. There's a little kink at Southeast 55th Avenue; veer right, then turn left again to stay on Hawthorne. (The small collection of buildings on your right at Southeast 56th Avenue make up the Portland campus of Western Seminary, an evangelical school.)

Just before reaching Southeast 50th Avenue you'll come to a couple of worthy stops, next door to each other on the left: ❶ **Albina Press,** where expert baristas churn out impeccable coffee in an open, gallery-like space (which in fact acts as a gallery, with art exhibitions that change once a month); and the ❷ **Sapphire Hotel,** a cozy, romantic wine bar with uncommonly attractive servers and a decadent opium-den feel. Both are excellent places to bring a date, if you're looking.

Now leave all that sophistication behind you, because you'll have no use for it on the block between Southeast 48th and 49th Avenues. This compact barhopping zone can do you serious damage if you're not careful: the establishments here are known (and sought out, especially by young 20-somethings and part-time pirates) for their liver-destroying qualities. Best to approach with caution. A good/terrible place to start is the ❸ **Space Room Lounge.** It's famous for hawking gigantic and needlessly robust Long Island iced tea in fishbowl glasses (if that tells you anything) and for the black-light murals of outer space that begin to look worryingly normal after a short time. Poke your head into a few of the other bars on the block, too, for future reference. (For an old-school unpretentious semipunk hangout, try ❹ **Bar of the Gods,** across the street.) And fear not: the next block holds several refueling options, including the rightly famous ❺ ¿Por Qué No? and the should-be-more-famous ❻ **East Side Deli.** Load up.

Continue making your perhaps-now-crooked way along Hawthorne. Crossing Southeast 39th Avenue, you'll see the ❼ **Hawthorne Theatre** building. These days it's a rock club, bar, and restaurant, but originally it was the Sunnyside Masonic Temple, built in 1919.

A densely packed shopping (and dining) strip extends from Southeast 39th Avenue down to about 32nd; here you'll find everything from beads to vintage furniture and clothing to quirky gifts. ❽ **Powell's Books** (whose main location takes up a whole downtown city block) has a store here, on the right near Southeast 37th Avenue, as well as an adjoining shop specializing in books for cooks and gardeners.

At Southeast 37th Avenue is a favorite Portland landmark, the ❾ **Bagdad Theater & Pub,** which more or less anchors this neighborhood. Built in 1927, partly funded by Universal Pictures, it's owned by the local McMenamins chain and shows first-run movies in addition to hosting various events, readings, lectures, and more. The onion-topped neon sign is a good indication of the awesome Mediterranean-style interior; few movie palaces from this era retain their original glory, but this one does. (Plus, if you duck around the corner of the theater on 37th Avenue, you'll find another bar in the same building: the adorable and tiny cigar bar Greater Trumps, which is worth checking out. If you're more hungry than thirsty, check out the Bread & Ink Cafe, a longstanding restaurant anchoring the next block.)

Continue wandering down Hawthorne Boulevard, investigating the various shops and restaurants as you see fit. Just past Southeast 31st Avenue you'll come to Hostelling International's ❿ **Hawthorne Portland Hostel,** a Hawthorne-ized bungalow from 1909 (dorm beds are $30–$40). The building has an ecoroof, a weird little clay-pagoda thing, and a stage in the huge backyard; it consistently wins sustainability awards, and it hosts a number of community-building events throughout the year (a bike-in movie night, travel-writing workshops, and the like). In contrast, a bit farther along, at Southeast 28th Avenue, you'll come to a hulking Safeway supermarket building that sticks out like a sore thumb in this bohemian neighborhood. The huge suburban fortress replaced a mid-1960s Safeway that had 20,000 fewer square feet and was certainly no beauty, but at least didn't impose itself on the surrounding blocks like an obnoxious beige-and-terra-cotta bully.

Backstory: Portland Adult Soapbox Derby

Held on the slopes of Mount Tabor, usually on a Saturday in mid-August, the Portland Adult Soapbox Derby is a favorite local tradition. The derby in its current incarnation started in 1997, inspired by a visit to San Francisco's annual Bernal Heights version. These days, thousands of spectators line the race course, brandishing tall cans of watery domestic beer as they loudly egg on the teams of racers. Forty-odd teams participate, building cars designed either for speed or for show (sometimes both). Themed cars have included a miniature Sandy Hut, complete with bartender; a fully lit stage with a band on it, performing all the way down the course; a tank; a rib cage; a kiddie pool; a big black Caddy; a taqueria serving tequila shots; a basketball court; a hot dog; and frequent winner Specific Gravity, which looks like a beautifully varnished handmade wooden kayak. The cars are powered by gravity only, and there's a limit to how much you can spend to build them (as well as rules about number of axles, type of wheels, allowable missiles, and so forth). Injuries are numerous and sometimes gruesome—epic road rash from being dragged down half the course beneath a car; a piece of flying metal to the face of a volunteer—but no one really complains. The derby's spirit is indomitable. The race usually lasts several hours, then culminates in a huge party somewhere near the foot of Mount Tabor. It's free to watch. If you're in town when it's on, don't miss it. For details, visit soapboxracer.com.

Moving quickly on, walk down the hill past the Holman Funeral Service building (from 1901 and very nice-looking) to reach **⓫ Excalibur Books & Comics,** one of the city's best comic-book shops. A few blocks down, at Southeast 23rd Avenue, is **⓬ Grand Central Bakery,** with a handful of locations around town and in Seattle; its rustic Como bread debuted in the late 1980s and basically educated Pacific Northwesterners about artisanal baking.

At Southeast 20th Avenue is yet another classic movie house, The **⓭ CineMagic,** a single-screen theater that opened in 1914. It's famous today for its teeny, adorable 1950s bathrooms and the awesome gold-lamé stage curtain (and, to some of us, for showing *The Secret of Roan Inish* for what seemed like decades but was really only about a year).

Continue down Hawthorne. On the left at 18th Avenue you'll see **⓮ Oui Presse,** an impeccably curated magazine store, gift shop, bakery, and coffee/tea/wine bar next door to the highly regarded restaurant **⓯ Castagna.** Ask about the bunny slippers!

Take a right onto Southeast 17th Avenue for one block. At Southeast 17th and Madison Street is the **⓰ Miao Fa Temple,** designed in 1926 by architect William Gray Purcell, who—not too surprisingly when you look at the building—once worked with Louis Sullivan, as well as other prominent Chicago architects. The building was originally a church but became a Buddhist temple in 1996. The more recently added Eastern-style embellishments (like bamboo roofing and the concrete lions guarding the entrance), juxtaposed with the clean-lined cube of the original building, make for a slightly trippy but somehow very pleasing sight.

Return to Hawthorne and take a right to continue west. At the corner of Southeast 12th Avenue and Hawthorne is one of the original trendsetting food-cart "pods" that have made Portland a destination for street food. Mainstays here include the great Potato Champion (in a word, poutine; in several words, late-night postbar poutine). This food-cart pod has a name (Cartopia) as well as beer, tents, and picnic tables. *Class!*

From here, it's a straight shot through lower Hawthorne to reach the Eastbank Esplanade. To get there, cross Southeast Grand Avenue and walk up onto the Hawthorne Bridge ramp as if you were going to cross the bridge. Just before the river, take the stairs down from the bridge onto the esplanade. (You could also simply walk

Bread and Ink Cafe, on the corner of Hawthorne a 36th Avenue, serves breakfast, lunch, and dinner.

toward the river at street level, underneath the bridge, but it's more fun to take the high road.)

To return to the starting point, retrace your steps across Southeast Grand Avenue and hop onto TriMet Bus 14, at Southeast Hawthorne Boulevard and Sixth Avenue.

Connecting the Walks

Follow Southeast 60th Avenue to meet up with **Walk 15: Stark-Belmont** (page 78). Hop off Hawthorne at Southeast Grand Avenue to join **Walk 12: Industrial Southeast** (page 59). At the Eastbank Esplanade, join **Walk 10: Hawthorne Bridge to Steel Bridge** (page 49).

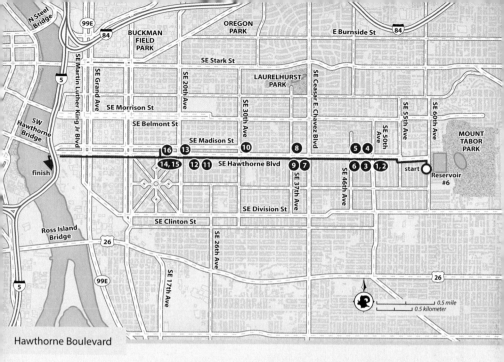

Hawthorne Boulevard

Points of Interest

1. Albina Press 5012 SE Hawthorne Blvd., 503-282-5214
2. Sapphire Hotel thesapphirehotel.com, 5008 SE Hawthorne Blvd., 503-232-6333
3. Space Room Lounge spaceroomlounge.com, 4800 SE Hawthorne Blvd., 503-235-6957
4. Bar of the Gods barofthegods.com, 4801 SE Hawthorne Blvd., 503-232-2037
5. ¿Por Qué No? porquenotacos.com, 4635 SE Hawthorne Blvd., 503-954-3138
6. East Side Deli pdxdeli.com, 4626 SE Hawthorne Blvd., 503-236-7313
7. Hawthorne Theatre hawthornetheatre.com, 1507 SE 39th Ave., 503-233-7100
8. Powell's Books powells.com, 3723 SE Hawthorne Blvd., 503-228-4651
9. Bagdad Theater & Pub mcmenamins.com/bagdad, 3702 SE Hawthorne Blvd., 503-467-7521
10. Hawthorne Portland Hostel portlandhostel.org, 3031 SE Hawthorne Blvd., 503-236-3380
11. Excalibur Books & Comics excaliburcomics.net, 2444 SE Hawthorne Blvd., 503-231-7351
12. Grand Central Bakery grandcentralbakery.com, 2230 SE Hawthorne Blvd., 503-445-1600
13. CineMagic Theater thecinemagictheater.com, 2021 SE Hawthorne Blvd., 503-231-7919
14. Oui Presse oui-presse.com, 1740 SE Hawthorne Blvd., 503-384-2160
15. Castagna castagnarestaurant.com, 1752 SE Hawthorne Blvd., 503-231-7373
16. Miao Fa Temple miaofatemple.com, 1722 SE Madison St., 503-239-5678

15 Stark-Belmont
Heart of the Southeast

Above: Horse Brass Pub has an authentic old-world feel.

BOUNDARIES: SE 60th Ave., SE Stark St., SE Belmont St., SE 20th Ave.
DISTANCE: 5 miles
DIFFICULTY: Easy (moderate if you include Mount Tabor)
PARKING: Free street parking
PUBLIC TRANSIT: TriMet Bus 15 runs along SE Belmont St. to and from downtown

Where do ordinary, average Portlanders hang out? Well, there's really no such thing as a typical Portlander, despite what a certain TV sketch-comedy series might have you believe, but this walk takes in a couple of residential neighborhoods that have a very Southeast Portland feel: moderate-size bungalows, nicely maintained yards with the occasional urban veggie farm or chicken coop, quiet tree-lined streets, chillaxed bars and restaurants where you can show up in jeans and not be looked at sideways. The houses are more modest as the street numbers get smaller (not counting one particularly ostentatious home we'll see). This is a nice walk to do in late afternoon or early evening, when it's not quite dark but the street life on Belmont is starting to pick up.

Walk Description

Start your walk at one of the oddest attractions in Portland: the ❶ **Zymoglyphic Museum.** It's a wonder cabinet of treasures crammed into the garage behind a house; just walking past, you'd never know it was there. But on the second and fourth Sunday of each month, the place opens to visitors, who will discover artifacts from a mysterious region: the Zymoglyphic, which exists mainly in the imagination of its creator, Jim Stewart. Stewart assembled most of the creations that fill the museum: terrariums showing typical scenes of life in the Zymoglyphic world, creatures who once inhabited its mossy landscapes, etc. It's a place well worth studying; just keep in mind, if you're bringing young kids, that the art and artifacts are fragile, so hands off.

At the corner of Southeast Belmont Street and 60th Avenue, you'll find the ❷ **Cheese Bar,** a deli and specialty-cheese shop with an impressive beer and wine list. Up the hill is Mount Tabor Park—if you have plenty of time, you might consider a picnic before you set out. Aside from being a wonderful place for a short hike, a picnic, walking your dog, training for bicycle races, or just lounging with a paperback, Mount Tabor also happens to be an extinct volcano, part of the Boring Lava Field. (We're not judging—that's what it's called.) The park includes about 190 acres atop the cinder cone, covered with leafy trees, ferns, reservoirs, and a network of trails (paved and unpaved), plus a well-maintained playground area. The many sets of stairs leading up to its top are popular with runners and masochists. The park is also the location of the annual Portland Adult Soapbox Derby (see Backstory on page 75). Fun fact: the hill is named after a Mount Tabor in Israel. Near the relatively flat top is a statue of Harvey Scott, who edited *The Oregonian* newspaper for several years starting in 1865. The statue was created by controversial sculptor Gutzon Borglum, whose credits include Mount Rushmore and early work on Georgia's Stone Mountain (which had financial backing from the Ku Klux Klan). In case you're the nervous type, fear not: the volcano hasn't been active for around 300,000 years, so you *should* be safe.

From the Cheese Bar, head west—downhill—along Southeast Belmont Street. Where the road bends at Southeast 55th Avenue, you'll see Mount Tabor Presbyterian Church, whose 100-year-old bell tower now houses ❸ **TaborSpace,** a nonprofit, pay-what-you-like coffee shop and community center. The big Arts and Crafts–style mansion on the right as you continue down the hill is the Blaine Smith House (5219 SE Belmont), built in 1909 and listed on the National Register of Historic Places. Note how the houses and yards become gradually less majestic as you make your way down the hill.

On your left, a few blocks farther down, is one of Portland's best-loved and most storied drinking establishments, the ❹ **Horse Brass Pub.** Its original publican, Don Younger, was crucial

Backstory: The Gardenburger

Given Portland's image in the popular imagination, it's probably not a huge surprise that the Gardenburger was invented here. (Strictly speaking, it happened in Gresham, but let's not quibble.) The meatless patty is the brainchild of Paul Wenner, who (after becoming concerned about what his lousy diet was doing to his mood, energy levels, and physical well-being) opened a vegetarian restaurant in 1981 called The Gardenhouse. Looking for something to do with all the leftovers one night, he made a probably not enormous intuitive leap and came up with the "Gardenloaf Sandwich." A little more fine-tuning (slice and fry, basically) converted the loafwich into an early version of the Gardenburger.

Customers at the Gardenhouse seemed to love it, but alas, the restaurant itself was not long for this world. Wenner closed up shop in the midst of a recession in 1984, but he was by no means out of the Gardenburger game. With financial backing from Harry Merlo, then CEO of Louisiana-Pacific, Wenner started Wholesome & Hearty Foods Inc. and continued to produce his trademark veggie burger.

The company changed its name to Gardenburger Inc. in 1985; it grew quickly and went public in 1992. Throughout the 1990s, competition from Boca Burgers, MorningStar Farms, and other companies following in Gardenburger's footsteps started picking up. Feeling the pressure, Gardenburger spent about $1.5 million on an advertising spot on the final episode of *Seinfeld*. Even so, the company continued losing money over the next few years: its stock prices dropped from $18 to 50 cents a share, and finally, in 2005, Gardenburger declared bankruptcy. Kellogg purchased the brand in 2007 and still owns it.

As for Wenner, he went on to write a couple of healthy-eating cookbooks and invented the Gardenbar, an early example of the now-ubiquitous savory vegan protein bar.

---

in the development of Portland's brewpub industry. The place has changed a bit since Younger's death in 2011 (following hard on the heels of Portland's smoking ban, which changed it almost as much—it was once known as by far the smokiest pub in town), but it's still reliably cozy and authentic, with darts and occasional live music. Pop in for a Scotch egg and one of the gazillion excellent beers on tap. The rough-hewn wooden tables and smoke-patinaed walls give the place a convincing old-world feel.

On the next block, just past the adorable, teeny-tiny Flipside Hats, is the city's coolest video store, ❺ **Movie Madness,** which doubles as a museum of film props and costumes. (Just how wide was Orson Welles in *Touch of Evil*? Take a look at his jacket on display here, and you'll have a pretty good idea. For fun, compare it to Erich von Stroheim's getup from *Sunset Boulevard,* or an itty-bitty outfit worn by Natalie Wood.) The video store was set to close when its owner, Mike Clark, announced his retirement at the end of 2017, but the nonprofit Hollywood Theatre (more about this in the Hollywood neighborhood walk, page 99) launched a successful campaign to raise money to rescue it. The purchase ensures that Portland won't lose this vast collection of titles—not to mention the museum pieces. The Hollywood also hopes to convert one room inside the video store into a screening room for special events.

Down the block and across the street is one of Portland's countless food-cart pods, where you can get anything from gyros to waffles to beer and cappuccino—even, as of this writing, a Norwegian *lefse*-meatball wrap.

At Southeast 42nd Avenue, hang a left, walk two blocks to Southeast Taylor Street, and turn right. Cross busy Southeast 39th Avenue, renamed Cesar E. Chavez Boulevard in 2009 (after a surprisingly long and contentious debate), and at Southeast 38th Avenue duck through a little alley to the left. Take a right at Southeast Main Street.

At the corner of Southeast Main and 36th Avenue is an uncharacteristically ostentatious house worth a peek. A pale-yellow Art Deco confection called the Deco Dream, it was built in 1992 by Paul Wenner, the man who invented the Gardenburger. (See Backstory: Gardenburger on opposite page.) Wenner has since sold the house, and it can now be rented through Airbnb, over-the-top deco details and all.

Take a right at Southeast 35th Avenue to get back onto Southeast Belmont Street, heading left (west). From about 35th to 33rd Avenues, Belmont coalesces into a lively, fun-filled hub of bars, coffee shops, and a nickel arcade with a cheap-movie theater attached (the ❻ **Avalon**, whose neon sign you can't miss). There's an artisan-cupcake shop; a range of cocktail lounges; a vegan bar in a former never-open mattress shop that everyone thought was a front for something shady; a bar named after Finnish designer Alvar Aalto; a gorgeously detailed old bungalow that houses beloved coffee shop the Pied Cow; and pizza. Explore!

Continue along Belmont Street. On your left, at Southeast 27th Avenue, note ❼ **Hanigan's Tavern**, which has long been affectionately and unofficially known as The Vern because most of the letters in its sign burned out ages ago; it's also one of the very cheapest drinkeries in town and one of the few remaining places that can legitimately be described as a dive.

At Southeast 20th Avenue you'll be facing Col. Summers Park, which in summer becomes a horrorscape of pasty-skinned Portlanders getting their first exposure to sunlight in many months, often while playing Frisbee or Hacky Sack (yes, the dream of the '90s really *is* alive in Portland). There's also a big patch of community gardens here. The park, established in 1938, is named after Col. Owen Summers, an Oregon legislator known for having commanded the Second Oregon Volunteers Regiment during the Spanish-American War.

Hang a right on Southeast 20th Avenue and cross Southeast Morrison Street; go right on Morrison, then, in half a block or so, duck left through the gate into ❽ **Lone Fir Pioneer Cemetery.** Founded in 1855, the cemetery started out as a farm; when the owner sold the land, his father was already buried here. Then a boiler explosion on a steamship belonging to the new owner, Colburn Barrell, killed several people, including Barrell's business partner, and he buried them all near the original tenant, starting what he called Mount Crawford Cemetery. In 1866 Barrell sold the land to a group of investors, and it was renamed Lone Fir for the one tree growing on the land. Now there are 25,000 people buried there, and a lot more than one tree. Like many urban cemeteries, it's a lovely, cool, quiet place to wander through. The area is fenced in, so aim diagonally for the gate at Southeast 26th Avenue, on the east side.

Exiting the cemetery, take a left at Southeast 26th Avenue, then a right at Southeast Stark Street. At Stark and Southeast 28th Avenue, you can link with Walk 17: Kerns and Laurelhurst Park, or you can continue up Stark, bordering Laurelhurst Park, along a quiet, tree-lined residential street.

At Stark and Southeast 43rd is a former Masonic lodge that is now headquarters of the Mazamas, an educational, nonprofit mountaineering group that organizes hikes, climbs, and classes—a great source of information if you're looking for local outdoor adventures.

Beer nerds should note ❾ **Belmont Station,** at Southeast Stark Street and 45th Avenue, a bottle shop with a pub attached. It's run by the same folks who operate the Horse Brass Pub. The variety of beer and hard cider available for purchase is astounding, as is the tap list, and a recent remodel means there's now a large patio out back, with sandwiches available from a local food cart.

The walk ends at ❿ **Caldera Public House,** a friendly brewpub serving upscale food and fine craft beers in the 1910 Thomas Graham building. It was once a pharmacy and is now a historic landmark, and once upon a time it faced a streetcar line that ran up and down the hill.

From Caldera, simply walk south on Southeast 60th Avenue to return to Southeast Belmont Street and our starting point.

Connecting the Walks

At Southeast 28th Avenue and Stark Street, you can link up with **Walk 17: Kerns and Laurelhurst Park** (page 89).

A sampling of the unique artifacts found at the Zymoglyphic Museum

Stark-Belmont

Points of Interest

1 Zymoglyphic Museum zymoglyphic.org/galleries.html, 6225 SE Alder St. (open second and fourth Sundays of the month)

2 Cheese Bar cheese-bar.com, 6031 SE Belmont St., 503-222-6014 (closed Mondays)

3 TaborSpace taborspace.org, 5441 SE Belmont St., 503-238-3904

4 Horse Brass Pub horsebrass.com, 4534 SE Belmont St., 503-232-2202

5 Movie Madness moviemadnessvideo.com, 4320 SE Belmont St., 503-234-4363

6 Avalon Theatre and Wunderland wunderlandgames.com, 3451 SE Belmont St., 503-238-1617

7 Hanigan's Tavern (aka The Vern) 2622 SE Belmont St., 503-233-7851

8 Lone Fir Pioneer Cemetery friendsoflonefircemetery.org, SE 26th Ave. between Stark and Morrison Sts.

9 Belmont Station belmont-station.com, 4500 SE Stark St., 503-232-8538

10 Caldera Public House calderapublichouse.com, 6031 SE Stark St., 503-233-8242

16 Montavilla
A Stark Story

Above: Over and Out, the semisecret bar hidden in the back of The Observatory restaurant and bar

BOUNDARIES: NE Hassalo St., 82nd Ave., SE Stark St., 75th Ave., NE Glisan St., NE 68th Ave.
DISTANCE: 3 miles
DIFFICULTY: Easy
PARKING: Free street parking
PUBLIC TRANSIT: TriMet Bus 15 (SE Stark St. and 80th Ave., SE Washington St. and 76th Ave.)

This up-and-coming little neighborhood, whose name is short for Mount Tabor Villa, has come a long way in recent years. Not too long ago it was at best neglected, at worst avoided, and even considered a little dodgy by many Portlanders. As recently as 2008, neighborhood complaints about prostitution problems in the neighborhood—primarily along 82nd Avenue—led the city to form a volunteer advisory committee of concerned citizens to look into eliminating the problem. Prostitution hasn't gone away completely, but things generally have been improving for Montavilla, at least in the neighborhood's main commercial core, which extends along Stark

Street from 76th Avenue to 82nd Avenue or so. The farmers market here is a big draw for locals as well as folks in other neighborhoods, as are several of the bars and restaurants that have opened up along here, not to mention the movie theater. Local residents have been lobbying for the past couple of years to establish a co-op grocery store in the area, not just for shopping but as an informal neighborhood community center where people could gather and meet each other; a volunteer organization called the Montavilla Food Co-Op has worked to raise funds and gather info to make the community-owned grocery store idea a reality here, and the project is in the location-scouting stage. Meanwhile, the whole area is just minutes from the top of Mount Tabor, an ideal playground and one of the city's best parks.

Walk Description

Start the walk at the site of the ❶ **Montavilla Farmers Market,** at the corner of Southeast 76th Avenue and Stark Street (note that it's open only on Sundays, 10 a.m.–2 p.m., June–October, plus a handful of dates throughout the winter months). Head west on Southeast Stark Street to 75th Avenue and turn right. Follow 75th several blocks until you reach Glisan Street, where you'll turn left. This little stretch of Glisan has a few appealing places to stop for refueling, including the old-school diner-lounge combo that is the ❷ **Candlelight** (recommended mostly for drinks and supercheap dive-bar breakfasts, FYI). But most of the businesses along here are strictly utilitarian: do your taxes, fix your car, buy some weed, or—for something a little different—pick up an authentic German pretzel at ❸ **Fressen Artisan Bakery.**

At Northeast 68th Avenue, turn right and go three blocks. At the corner of Northeast 68th and Hassalo Street you'll come to a sign for the 2-acre Rosemont Bluff Natural Area, a sort of buffer zone of undeveloped woodland and wildlife habitat covering a steep slope. It's naturally populated with Douglas-fir and maple, but invasive ivy and blackberry plants are a constant problem, so neighbors volunteer frequently to help maintain the park. (This neighborhood is technically not part of Montavilla but rather North Tabor or Center; *Center* started out as an acronym that stood for Citizens Engaged Now Towards Ecological Review.)

After exploring the bluff, go back to the entrance and head east on Northeast Hassalo Street. At Northeast 76th Avenue, turn right. Turn left on Northeast Irving Street; walk a block, then turn left again on Northeast 78th Avenue, and then turn right on Northeast Oregon Street. Where Oregon meets Northeast 82nd Avenue, you'll come to ❹ **Milepost 5**, a cool multiuse space that incorporates live/work art studios and galleries. Stroll the complex, taking in the artwork, or check the website for a calendar of performances and events being held in the theater space.

Turn right on Northeast 82nd Avenue, one of the least glamorous streets in Portland—all fast-food restaurants, gas stations, and cheap motels. At the corner of Northeast Glisan Street is one welcome exception: the ❺ **Montavilla Community Center**. It has two outdoor pools, a basketball court, meeting rooms, classrooms, and a varied program of activities for both kids and adults.

Continue along 82nd Avenue, taking care not to make eye contact with passing cars lest they mistake you for someone selling one or another category of illicit goods and services. Just as you begin to suspect that you're trudging headlong into Portland's used-car-sales territory, you'll come to Southeast Stark Street. Turn right onto Stark. There's a semisecret neighborhood bar nearby—or, to be more precise, a neighborhood bar with a semisecret entrance; to find it, traverse the McDonald's parking lot and walk around to the back of the building next door, until you

Academy Theater offers beer and pizza along with second-run movies.

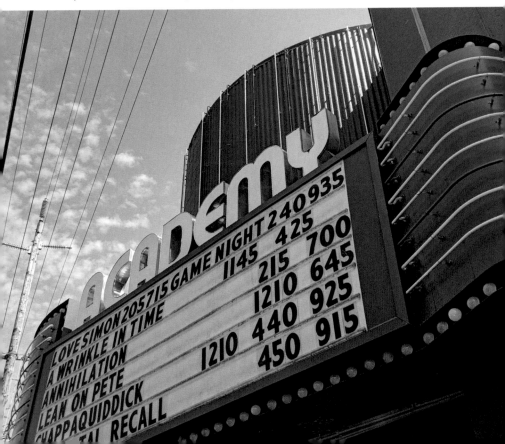

come to a glass door. This is the **6** **Over and Out,** the back bar hidden behind a more upscale neighborhood restaurant and cocktail bar called **6** **The Observatory.** (You could also go in the front door on Stark Street, and walk through the restaurant to the back, but that's somehow less exciting.) The Over and Out is a boxy, relaxed space with pool tables and pinball, an excellent cocktail menu, and several of the same food items you can get in the restaurant (plus a great happy-hour selection).

Continue to make your way along Southeast Stark Street, which as you'll notice is a small but expanding commercial stretch, with fancy new cocktail lounges and bottle shops mixed in among places that have been here since before it was cool, like **7** **Portland Tub and Tan.** (Hot tubs by the hour? Nothing sketchy about that whatsoever!) On the right, just before Southeast 80th Avenue, is **8** **Ya Hala Lebanese Restaurant,** an excellent choice if you're hungry; it was one of the first restaurants to be established along this stretch. Next door to it, and owned by the same friendly family, is a small international grocery and supplies store, where you can get orange-flower water, gorgeous-smelling olive soap, Mediterranean cooking supplies, cheese, tea and spices, baked goods, and many other things.

In the next block of Stark is **9** **The Country Cat,** one of the first restaurants here to get attention from folks outside the neighborhood. The family-owned place serves snazzed-up home-style American classics for dinner nightly, but it's perhaps even more universally loved as a brunch spot. At the end of the block is the **10** **Bipartisan Cafe,** a stellar coffee shop that also makes fantastic pies and pastries. Like pretty much all of the businesses on this stretch, both of these places are noticeably kid-friendly; The Country Cat has a children's menu, and the Bipartisan has a play corner and is usually full of at least as many strollers as laptops. It also has great pie and a fascinating collection of sociopolitical posters, newspapers, memorabilia, and art on the walls.

Diagonally across the street from the Bipartisan is another of Portland's great beer-and-pizza second-run movie houses, the **11** **Academy Theater.** Built originally in 1948 as a single-screen theater, it had been closed and languishing since the 1970s before it was bought, restored, and reopened in 2006 as a multiscreen second-run theater and pub. (Along with 10 microbrews on tap, the theater serves pizza from the next-door **12** **Flying Pie Pizzeria,** an old-school favorite.) It's both kid- and parent-friendly: before 8 p.m. the theater offers babysitting services, which means you only have to watch that Disney-princess movie if you *really* want to.

Walk another block or so along Southeast Stark Street to return to the farmers market and the route's starting point.

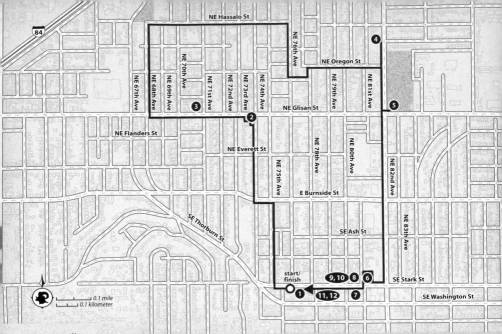

Montavilla

Points of Interest

1 Montavilla Farmers Market montavillamarket.org, 7600 block of SE Stark St.

2 Candlelight Restaurant & Lounge 7334 NE Glisan St., 503-253-9738

3 Fressen Artisan Bakery fressenartisanbakery.com, 7075 NE Glisan St., 503-953-3222

4 Milepost 5 milepost5.net, 850 NE 81st Ave.

5 Montavilla Community Center 8219 NE Glisan St., 503-823-4101

6 Over and Out/The Observatory theobservatorypdx.com, 410 SE 81st Ave., 503-445-6284

7 Portland Tub and Tan tubandtan.com, 8028 SE Stark St., 503-261-1180

8 Ya Hala Lebanese Restaurant yahalarestaurant.com, 8005 SE Stark St., 503-256-4484

9 The Country Cat thecountrycat.net, 7937 SE Stark St., 503-408-1414

10 Bipartisan Cafe bipartisancafe.com, 7901 SE Stark St., 503-253-1051

11 Academy Theater academytheaterpdx.com, 7818 SE Stark St., 503-252-0500

12 Flying Pie Pizzeria flying-pie.com, 7804 SE Stark St., 503-254-2016

17 Kerns and Laurelhurst Park
The Bermuda Triangle

Above: A mansion in the tree-lined neighborhood surrounding Laurelhurst Park

BOUNDARIES: SE Cesar Chavez Blvd., SE Stark St., NE 15th Ave., NE Sandy Blvd.
DISTANCE: 3.5 miles
DIFFICULTY: Easy
PARKING: Free street parking
PUBLIC TRANSIT: TriMet Bus 75 (SE Cesar Chavez Blvd. and Ash St.)

There are enough entertaining diversions on this walk that you may well never return from it. The route starts and stops at one of Portland's finest green spaces, the beautifully landscaped Laurelhurst Park. Surrounding the park are block after block of sturdy, dignified old houses on gently curving, tree-lined streets. From here we'll make a vaguely triangular path that swings through the Kerns neighborhood's miniature Restaurant Row, along 28th Avenue, then down along a relatively unglamorous stretch of lower Sandy Boulevard that has seen a lot of recent development but is still home to at least one scruffy, well-loved dive bar. (Sensitive readers should note that there may be a small detour into nostalgia when we get to this part.) The third side of our lopsided triangle will be formed by East Burnside Street, one of the city's main east–west arteries and a constantly evolving business corridor, which among many other things is the site of an excellent movie theater and pub.

Walk Description

Start at the bus stop at Southeast 39th Avenue (aka Cesar Chavez Boulevard) and Ash Street. Take the paved path into the park toward the lake, following the part that veers off to the left. Laurelhurst Park covers about 26 acres and once belonged to William Ladd, the same former mayor responsible for Ladd's Addition (see Backstory: William S. Ladd on page 69). The park was designed in 1912, and in 2001 it became the first city park in the US to be listed on the National Register of Historic Places. The spring-fed central pond started out as a watering hole for cattle; for several years, an angry swan named General Pershing lorded over it. These days it's a great place to see baby ducks in spring (don't feed them). There are picnic spots scattered around, an off-leash dog run area, and gently hilly paved trails great for jogging. (Or, you know, walking.)

Follow the path around the lake and on through the middle of the park until it bumps into Southeast 33rd Avenue; turn right onto 33rd. At the top of the short hill, turn left onto Southeast Ankeny Street, then right at Southeast 32nd Avenue. Where 32nd meets East Burnside Street, you'll find ❶ **Music Millennium,** an independent record store that has been a vital piece of the Portland music scene for decades (it was founded in 1969). Its larger outpost in Northwest Portland closed in 2007, but this location (the original) is still kicking, hosting frequent in-store performances and an annual Customer Appreciation BBQ.

Turn left on East Burnside Street and head down the hill. At Northeast 28th Avenue, take a right. Between East Burnside and Northeast Glisan Streets along 28th is a strip of bars and restaurants of surprising range, from a small-plates wine bar to upscale diner food to gelato and gourmet chocolate. On the corner at Glisan Street is ❷ **Pambiche,** whose vivid color scheme means you can't miss it; it's an always-packed, extremely cheerful Cuban restaurant.

At Northeast Glisan Street, turn left. For an incredibly glamorous version of the street you're now walking down, seek out indie-film director Aaron Katz's 2010 movie *Cold Weather,* shot in Portland; it makes Glisan Street and various other parts of the city seem lit from within, despite (or maybe because of) the gray skies and damp asphalt. The big brick apartment building on your left, called the Rasmussen, plays a pivotal role in *Cold Weather* (though it appears under an alias).

There's a little curl at the end of Glisan Street where it meets Northeast 22nd Avenue and Sandy Boulevard. Note the pawn shop at this corner. Until noise complaints from neighbors forced it to close in December 2000, this building held one of the all-time great rock clubs,

EJ's—a grimy little den that rivaled Satyricon and LaLuna for the allegiance of the city's music scensters in the 1990s. (EJ's was a strip club until 1994, when the owner switched to live music; neighbors made remarkably little fuss over *that* transformation.)

On the other side of Northeast Sandy Boulevard is a big empty space in the heart of every Portland barfly: the site of the late, lamented Club 21, where you'd go for cheap drinks between the bands at EJ's. It closed in January 2017, and the castle-shaped building was torn down to make room for new mixed-use construction. (Club 21's owners briefly toyed with the idea of putting the little hut on a barge somehow and running it as a floating bar, but this turned out to be impractical.)

Cross Northeast Sandy Boulevard and continue straight (north) along 22nd Avenue for three blocks. Here you'll find some consolation for all the city's lost dive bars, in the form of a truly excellent brewpub: ❸ **Culmination Brewing**, whose brief food menu is nearly as inventive as its beer list. If the peach sour is on tap, try it, even if you don't think you like sour beers. Trust me.

Retracing your steps along Northeast 22nd Avenue back to Northeast Sandy Boulevard, take a right. At Northeast 17th Avenue you'll come to ❺ **See See Motor Coffee Co.**, an impeccably stylish coffee bar and motorcycle-friendly hangout-shop that's well worth venturing into (it sells Bell helmets, riding gear for men and women, imported magazines, some outdoor apparel, rugged camping gear, and more). Make sure you get a good look at the espresso machine, painted with psychedelic-wizard van art. See See is also the force behind the annual One Moto Show, a

Laurelhurst Park, the first city park in the country to be listed on the National Register of Historic Places

massive motorcycle-themed art show, trade show, and party that draws thousands of bike fans to the city each winter.

Continue along Northeast Sandy Boulevard. Where Sandy crosses Northeast Davis Street you'll see the Eastside outpost of ❻ **Voodoo Doughnut,** looking reliably hideous in its Pepto Bismol–lite color scheme (though much, much less crowded than its downtown sibling, in case you're desperate to tell folks back home that you tried a bacon-maple bar).

Take a left at Northeast 15th Avenue, just in front of the wedge-shaped ❼ **Sandy Hut,** another of the city's best (diviest? oldest) dive bars. A 1920s steakhouse, the Hut recently benefited from a tasteful makeover courtesy of the owners of Club 21. They basically peeled off a few layers to reveal the building's original details, like a strip of stained glass around the edge and a wall of glass bricks in one corner. The basic menu has retro touches (including a burger first served here in the 1960s) and theme nights; come in on Wednesdays for a hefty prime rib dinner. (Until recently the neon sign promised STEAMED CLAMS, but these, sadly, are no longer available.) There's pinball in the back, and on one wall is a fading but still lovely replica of an Al Hirschfeld drawing—entertain yourself by searching for the name Nina, which Hirschfeld hid in many of his pieces in honor of his daughter (there are supposedly three here, but your intrepid guide has only ever seen two).

Dragging yourself reluctantly away from the Hut, continue along Northeast 15th Avenue and turn left on East Burnside Street. At Northeast 22nd Avenue you'll find one of Portland's coffee labs: ❽ **Heart Roasters,** an industrial-chic hangout that opened in 2009 as part of the wave of post-Stumptown seriousness regarding the art and science of caffeination.

Continue up East Burnside Street to Northeast 28th Avenue, where you will find the excellent ❾ **Laurelhurst Theater.** The Art Deco theater opened in 1923 as a single-screen movie house but now has several auditoriums and serves beer, wine, and pizza. It spent decades as a second-run and revival house, but has now begun showing first-run movies—movies with all-day matinee prices on Tuesdays.

Turn right on Southeast 28th Avenue, passing another classic old-Portland bar, Holman's, worth a stop if you're peckish—then turn left on Southeast Ankeny Street. Follow Ankeny past Southeast 33rd Avenue (where you exited the park earlier); glance to your right as you pass two old-Portland mansions looming on their small hillside. Stay on Southeast Ankeny Street until you reach the park entrance, just before Southeast Laurelhurst Place, and then take a right into the park. Follow the main path back through Laurelhurst Park to the starting point.

Kerns and Laurelhurst Park

Points of Interest

1. **Music Millennium** musicmillennium.com, 3158 E. Burnside St., 503-231-8926

2. **Pambiche** pambiche.com, 2811 NE Glisan St., 503-233-0511

3. **Culmination Brewing** culminationbrewing.com, 2117 NE Oregon St., 971-254-9114

4. **See See Motor Coffee Co.** seeseemotorcycles.com, 1642 NE Sandy Blvd., 503-894-9566

5. **Voodoo Doughnut** voodoodoughnut.com, 1501 NE Davis St., 503-235-2666

6. **The Sandy Hut** sandyhut.com, 1430 NE Sandy Blvd., 503-235-7972

7. **Heart Roasters** heartroasters.com, 2211 E. Burnside St., 503-206-6602

8. **Laurelhurst Theater** laurelhursttheater.com, 2735 E. Burnside St., 503-232-5511

18 Irvington
The Beautiful and the Damned

Above: A fairy-tale cottage at the corner of 28th Avenue and U. S. Grant Place

BOUNDARIES: NE Knott St., NE Weidler St., NE 15th Ave., NE 28th Ave.
DISTANCE: 2.5 miles
DIFFICULTY: Easy
PARKING: Free street parking
PUBLIC TRANSIT: TriMet Bus 8 (NE 15th Ave. and Broadway), MAX Red and Blue Lines (Lloyd Center)

Irvington was planned, successfully, as an upper-middle-class neighborhood, with strict rules about things like yard size and the proximity of sidewalks to front doors. There was also, for a long time, a rule against most commercial development, which in hindsight was a great idea, as it has allowed much of the neighborhood to be preserved as originally laid out: quiet, tree-lined streets with big, stately houses and well-landscaped yards. (This is not counting the parts that were demolished to build up the Lloyd District—more on that later.) Irvington is a pleasure to walk through, despite the lack of things to do here. This walk is mostly just a peaceful wander among the lovely old Victorian houses, with a couple of exceptions, and one jarring architectural and spiritual contrast that couldn't be avoided. (Spoiler alert: it's a mall.)

Walk Description

Start the walk at the corner of Northeast 15th Avenue and Broadway. Head north along 15th. As you cross Northeast Schuyler Street you'll see an enormous sky-blue Queen Anne house, which is the friendly and beloved ❶ **Lion and the Rose Victorian Bed & Breakfast** (fans of the NBC series *Grimm,* set and filmed in Portland, might recognize it from an episode in Season 1).

Continue along Northeast 15th Avenue to Northeast Thompson Street, where you'll turn right. Walk a block, then turn left onto Northeast 16th Avenue. Follow 16th to Northeast Brazee Street, where you have an opportunity for refreshment at the ❷ **15th Avenue Hophouse.** Dozens of imported and craft beers are available here, along with some killer sweet potato fries and other classed-up pub fare. It almost didn't open, which is surprising in light of its quiet, low-key, grown-up vibe. The Irvington Community Association voted in early 2011 not to grant the pub a liquor license, citing concerns about noise. (The president of the association told *The Oregonian* afterward that he thought the opposition was "generational.") That vote meant that the pub would be allowed to serve beer and wine but not be granted a full liquor license. But a good-neighbor agreement in the wake of the vote helped the two parties iron out their differences, and the pub opened with a full license and a lot of vocal support from neighbors.

Continue along Northeast 16th Avenue to Northeast Knott Street, and turn right. From Knott, take a right on Northeast 20th Avenue. At Northeast Thompson Street turn left and continue several blocks, then turn right at Northeast 28th Avenue.

At the corner of Northeast 28th Avenue and U. S. Grant Place is an adorable cottage (OK, it's huge for a cottage, but it looks distinctly hobbity) that stands out even in a neighborhood full of pretty houses. Note the extra-cool spiderweb glass in one small window.

Keep walking down Northeast 28th Avenue another block, then turn right onto Northeast Tillamook Street. Go left at Northeast 27th Avenue, then right onto Northeast Hancock Street for a block, then left onto Northeast 26th Avenue, then right into the Hancock Street–Broadway Alley. Portland has a number of these unmaintained alleyways; they're public rights-of-way and open to (slow-moving) traffic, though often unpaved and challenging for cars. Mostly they're a fun way to see a neighborhood from a new angle: namely, the back door.

Exiting the alley, take a right onto Northeast 25th Avenue, then a left on Northeast Hancock Street. At the corner of Hancock and Northeast 22nd Avenue is ❸ **Portland's White House,** a

Backstory: Oregon Convention Center

A few blocks southwest of the Lloyd Center mall is the Oregon Convention Center, easily spotted from anywhere near the river by its twin green-tinted glass spires. Opened in 1990 and renovated in 2003, the convention center encompasses almost a million square feet and covers the equivalent of 14–16 city blocks. It's owned by Metro (the regional government) and operated by a Metro subsidiary called MERC (Metropolitan Exposition Recreation Commission).

The convention center management prides itself on keeping the building green and energy-efficient; in 2004 the OCC became the first convention center anywhere to be awarded a LEED certification from the U.S. Green Building Council, and in 2014 it was bumped up to LEED Platinum. It's filled with public art and interesting, practical features such as, for example, the rainwater garden in the southwest corner of the center. The rainwater garden, officially certified Salmon-Safe in 2007, collects water from the roof of the building, then channels it along an artificial stream made to look like a real one, with native plants along its edges. Terraced pools slow down the water and filter out sediment; this system of treating the runoff saves the convention center around 1.2 million gallons a year, according to its website, and it reduces landscaping costs as well.

Public art in the building includes the world's largest bronze Foucault pendulum, weighing 900 pounds and measuring 36 inches across; a 40-foot-long red dragon boat built in Taiwan, commemorating the dragon boat races held each year during Portland's Rose Festival; and the giant hanging sculpture *Ginkgoberry Gwa* by New York City artist Ming Fay, with its enormous red-glass blossoms and gnarled roots. A brand-new, 600-room hotel adjoining the Convention Center was partially complete at the time of this writing.

---

luxury bed-and-breakfast in a historic, gorgeously renovated Victorian building that, if you squint, really does look a little bit like that other White House.

Turn left on Northeast 22nd, then right on Northeast Broadway, the neighborhood's main drag. You'll find any number of eating and drinking options along this stretch; I recommend the ❹ Rose & Thistle, fondly known as the RAT, for a cozy neighborhood pub atmosphere. Its back patio has heated booths and a garden feel, and the pints of Guinness meet the approval of a wide swath of expats from across the pond. Just before Northeast 17th Avenue is the excellent ❺ Broadway Books, an independent bookstore that holds frequent events and author appearances. The store is a particularly active supporter of regional authors, such as Chelsea Cain (*Heartsick*), Cheryl Strayed (*Wild*), and Willy Vlautin (*Lean on Pete*). The staff is known for above-and-beyond customer service.

Follow Northeast Broadway to Northeast 15th Avenue, passing the route's starting point, crossing 15th and turning left. Turn right at Northeast Halsey (by the Applebee's, a harbinger if ever there was one), then left down the unlovely concrete path through the **❻ Lloyd Center** mall parking lot.

Lloyd Center was a $100 million, 1.2-million-square-foot project when it opened in August 1960. (It was designed by architect John Graham, who also designed Seattle's Space Needle.) At the time it was considered a shining achievement in architecture, which is sort of astounding to contemplate when you look at it today. Of course, this was before the entire place was boxed in with a light-killing roof and, later, plastered end-to-end in grayish-beige carpet. The original design was for an open-air mall and community center, with fountains and sculptures amid the shops, large windows everywhere, and of course the crown jewel, a skating rink. (This rink, by the way, is one of the places where bad-girl Olympic figure skater–turned–boxer–turned–movie heroine Tonya Harding used to practice.) In old photos, Lloyd Center actually does look quite attractive, with its water features and its airy spiral staircases lifting shoppers

Portland's White House, a B&B located in a renovated Victorian building

toward unlimited retail delights. But the mall was sold in 1986 and renovated into its boxy shape in 1990. (And by the way, in focusing on its terrible aesthetics, we're overlooking the mall's previous crimes: its construction involved the razing of several residential blocks, and its popularity helped sap downtown of its draw as a retail destination.) The good news is that a new renovation is in the works, and the drawings indicate that it's likely to be a drastic improvement, spanning five years and costing somewhere in the realm of $100 million. The new plan includes architectural nods to the original, open-air design of the building. One part of the redo will be a massive food court on the lower level of the mall, with outlets of some of the city's most popular local restaurants (rather than the depressing range of fast-food options typical of most malls).

Back away slowly from the mall, turn left on Northeast 15th Avenue, and retrace your steps up to Northeast Broadway to return to the walk's starting point.

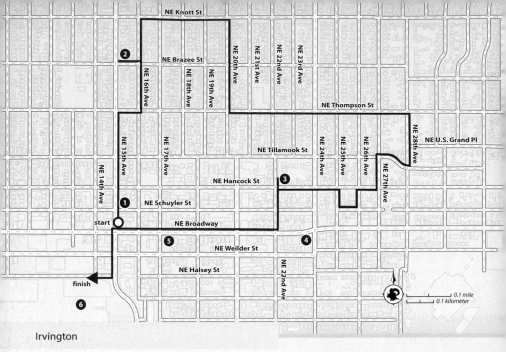

Irvington

Points of Interest

1 **Lion and the Rose Victorian Bed & Breakfast** lionrose.com, 1810 NE 15th Ave., 503-287-9245

2 **15th Avenue Hophouse** oregonhophouse.com, 1517 NE Brazee St., 971-266-8392

3 **Portland's White House** portlandswhitehouse.com, 1914 NE 22nd Ave., 503-287-7131

4 **Rose & Thistle** roseandthistlepdx.com, 2314 NE Broadway, 503-287-8582

5 **Broadway Books** broadwaybooks.net, 1714 NE Broadway, 503-284-1726

6 **Lloyd Center** lloydcenter.com, 2201 Lloyd Center, 503-282-2511

19 Hollywood
Almost Famous

Above: Outdoor retailer the Mountain Shop occupies a former dairy bottling plant.

BOUNDARIES: NE 52nd Ave., NE Halsey St., NE 37th Ave., NE Brazee St.
DISTANCE: 2 miles
DIFFICULTY: Easy
PARKING: Free street parking
PUBLIC TRANSIT: TriMet Bus 12 (NE 42nd Ave. and Sandy Blvd.), MAX Green, Red and Blue Lines and
    Buses 66, 75, and 77 (Hollywood/NE 42nd Ave. Transit Center)

Anchored by a fabulous old movie theater but otherwise pretty much unrelated to that other Hollywood, this is a fun little neighborhood that could be easily overlooked if you didn't know better. Until recently, it was often thought of as a place you go through on your way to somewhere else. TriMet has a transit center here, with several light-rail and bus lines converging, so it's a key point for public transit. Plus, auto-worshiping Sandy Boulevard cuts right through the middle of it at a diagonal, and some of the resulting intersections will make you glad you're

Backstory: Grindhouse Film Festival

One of the coolest things about the Hollywood Theatre is the Grindhouse Film Festival, which, though it started as an annual festival, is a monthly series programmed by Dan Halsted, the theater's head programmer. Halsted has a vast collection of obscure, usually one-of-a-kind 35mm prints of some of the craziest movies you've never heard of, as well as all the best and weirdest of the classic Hong Kong action films. He's a serious archivist, refreshingly free of irony—you don't go to Grindhouse screenings to feel all smarty-pants-cooler-than-the-movie; you go because the movies are sincerely awesome. (If you're familiar with the work of the Alamo Drafthouse, the Grindhouse Film Fest is along those same lines; Halsted and the Alamo guys are pals.) Halsted is also something of a celluloid-treasure hunter, traveling far and wide in search of lost and neglected movies—years ago he found a huge stash of vintage kung fu films stored beneath an old theater in Vancouver, British Columbia, that had been closed since 1985.

Halsted screens something under the Grindhouse brand about once a month, and it's always worth checking out, though some of these lost treasures are better than others. (*Five Element Ninjas:* YES. *Miami Connection?* Well ... yes, too, but maybe not for everybody.) He also does an annual (or thereabouts) evening of movie trailers from the 1970s and '80s that is surprisingly entertaining and wildly popular. For both, advance tickets are recommended.

For details of what's coming up soon, check out grindhousefilmfest.com or hollywoodtheatre.org.

walking rather than driving. New businesses have been filling in storefronts along the main drag and a few side streets, adding new life to the area. But a few steps off Sandy, the streets are mostly quiet and the atmosphere laid-back. It's a good in-between-things 'hood, close to several other parts of town, but Hollywood has come into its own as a destination in recent years. You'll want to stay awhile.

Walk Description

Start at the Hollywood/Northeast 42nd Avenue Transit Center, where the MAX light-rail line stops. Leaving the train platform, turn left (north) on the pedestrian bridge and continue straight along Northeast 42nd Avenue. At Northeast Broadway, hang a left; note the excellent 1950s neon sign for ❶ Chin's Kitchen Chinese restaurant. For years, the sign was the best thing about Chin's, but the restaurant recently changed ownership and instantly won the hearts of persnickety locals and food writers alike; if you're not quite hungry yet, keep it in mind for later.

Where Broadway meets Northeast Sandy Boulevard, you'll see a yellow metal sculpture of a pair of vintage eyeglasses, lending its (by now rather faded) version of glamour to the neighborhood.

Veer left onto Northeast Sandy and follow it a few blocks to where it meets Northeast Halsey Street. For a few years in the early 2000s, the triangle-shaped corner building was home to The Blackbird, a short-lived but fondly remembered rock club of the sort that has all but disappeared, at least in Portland: small and cozy, with affordable door prices and zero pretension, but whose management was well connected enough to book touring indie bands you'd actually heard of, bands that usually played much bigger venues. Later it became Tony Starlight's, a Vegas-style supper club and lounge that was one of the few Portland venues with a dress code. After that, the space was transformed into the second incarnation of another beloved rock club, The Know, which had been a mainstay on Northeast Alberta Street for a decade, until rent increases drove it away. The new Know lasted just over a year in its Sandy Boulevard spot before closing suddenly amid a management dispute. But all is not lost: in September 2018 the space reopened as a pinball-focused dive bar called ❷ **Wedge Head,** with dozens of the most sought-after machines and cool murals by local artists on the walls, and your author could not be more delighted.

Diagonally across Sandy Boulevard is what used to be known as the 7-Up Building, although these days its bottle-shaped tower has a real-estate company's sign where the neon 7-Up sign used to be. (Inside is the ❸ **Mountain Shop,** an excellent place to stock up on outdoor gear and supplies for hiking, climbing, and camping, with helpful salespeople who are great at answering questions and making unbiased suggestions.) Before its decades-long run as the 7-Up Building (which lasted from the 1940s through 2002), this was the Steigerwald Dairy bottling plant, and the current cylindrical tower was actually milk-bottle-shaped. (The original bottle is still there, inside and underneath the cylinder, like a huge Russian nesting doll, and allegedly it can be glimpsed if you peek through the windows from the proper angle in just the right light.) The dairy opened in 1926 and was one of the first places to set up an automated bottling process. Its 75-foot-high tower was the tallest building in Portland for a while. The dairy closed in 1936, and the tower took on its new shape shortly thereafter.

Backtrack up Northeast Sandy to Northeast 40th Avenue, where you'll take a left over to Northeast Hancock Street. At the corner is a great refueling spot inside the old public library building: ❹ **Fleur de Lis,** an artisan bakery run by Greg Mistell, who used to manage the Hollywood Farmers Market and, more to the point, once owned Pearl Bakery. It's very kid-friendly and famous for the enormous cinnamon rolls—*The Oregonian* called them the best in Portland, and they're surely the biggest. The Fleur de Lis also supplies its bread to several of the city's best sandwich shops. Keep in mind that this is a popular neighborhood stop, so if you want the best selection of pastries, or a place to sit, get here early.

Keep going up Northeast 40th Avenue toward Northeast Tillamook Street. On your left, where there is now a McDonald's, was the late, lamented Yaw's Top Notch Restaurant, a beloved drive-in burger joint that thrived during the sudden boom of car culture along Sandy Boulevard in the 1950s and '60s. Yaw's was one of the key stops for guys and dolls out cruisin' on a Saturday night. As the story goes, a traffic cop used to keep the wild youngsters in line by handing out Tootsie Rolls. Yaw's closed in 1982, after 56 years; an attempt to revive it in another location, several blocks east in the Gateway neighborhood, didn't last, and it closed for good in 2013.

At Northeast Tillamook Street, turn right to pass the Multnomah County Library; this branch is another example of the library's participation in innovatively designed multiuse buildings, incorporating shops and affordable living spaces.

At Northeast 42nd Avenue take another right. Here you'll find one of the nicest European-style pubs in town: **5** **The Moon and Sixpence,** with a great beer and whiskey selection, excellent fish-and-chips, darts, occasional acoustic music, authentically carpeted floors, and a huge back patio. If you didn't bring anything to read, you can borrow a battered volume from one of their crowded shelves.

Continuing along Northeast 42nd Avenue, you'll notice on the left another of the neighborhood's little nods to its namesake: a Hollywood-star sculpture–cum–bicycle rack at Northeast Hancock Street. Turn right on Hancock then left on Northeast 41st Avenue to admire the cheesy but charming murals gracing the exterior of **6** **Sam's Billiards.** Sam's itself is a sort of disco-sleazy pool hall, well worth investigating if you're into that sort of thing (and who isn't, really?). Pool tables rent by the hour.

Heading back toward Sandy Boulevard, you'll see the impressive facade of the **7** **Hollywood Theatre.** The Hollywood opened in 1926, back when a streetcar line ran up Sandy and this part of town was far enough away from downtown Portland to count as an excursion. The theater was an immediate hit. People showed up in droves, and the theater ended up giving the neighborhood its name (and, if you ask us, most of its enduring

The neighborhood's namesake

character, even today). The place struggled to hold on through the 1980s and '90s, but it was rescued in 1997 by Film Action Oregon, a nonprofit that has been gradually restoring the interior while transforming the place into an educational resource for film lovers. (See Backstory: Grindhouse Film Festival, page 100.) It's one of the few cinemas left in town—or anywhere, really—that regularly shows movies on 35mm and even, occasionally, 70mm film rather than in digital format, and the programming never fails to be interesting (now with beer!). It's largely volunteer-run, and the organization's educational arm does things like putting pro-level equipment in the hands of talented young kids who want to make documentaries, or bringing animation classes to junior high schools, so you can feel good about springing for a ticket to see *The Thin Man* on the big screen with a pint of Laurelwood red ale on a Sunday afternoon.

Turn left to continue up Sandy. At Northeast 42nd Avenue is the very cute ❽ **Reo's Ribs,** formerly the Hollywood Burger Bar and once upon a time a streetcar-ticket-sales office. At the time of this writing, it was still boarded up after a fire. But plans were moving forward to reopen, and a sign hanging out front promised, "We will be back!" The place is co-owned by Reo Varnado, who also happens to be Snoop Dogg's uncle.

If you're walking on a Saturday, take a right at Northeast Hancock Street and browse the busy ❾ **Hollywood Farmers Market** (May–October), in the parking lot between Northeast 44th and 45th Avenues. It's one of the bigger and more established markets in Portland.

Backtrack north (left) on Northeast 45th Avenue to return to Sandy. Continue right and up the hill. If you're hungry by now, and you didn't stop for ribs, there's a food cart on the left called the ❿ **Whole Bowl,** serving superhealthy bowls of veggies on brown rice.

Or maybe something a little more indulgent is in order. Nearing the top of the hill is ⓫ **Laurelwood Public House,** a great brewery with awesome beer that serves as a gathering spot for parents—it's known for being kid-friendly. But first, take a scenic detour to really earn your beer: at 47th, hang a left, then a right at Brazee, and a left at 49th, which takes you up a small ridge full of very pretty houses. Turn right at the top (Northeast Wistaria Drive), and then head down the staircase to your right—technically 50th Avenue but mostly just a prettier route back to Sandy Boulevard. Turn left at Sandy and rest your legs with a nice pint at Laurelwood.

From here you can catch Bus 12 toward downtown, which stops at 42nd and Sandy, about a block from the bus/light-rail station where the walk started.

Connecting the Walks

This walk can be extended to join **Walk 20: Upper Sandy** (page 105)

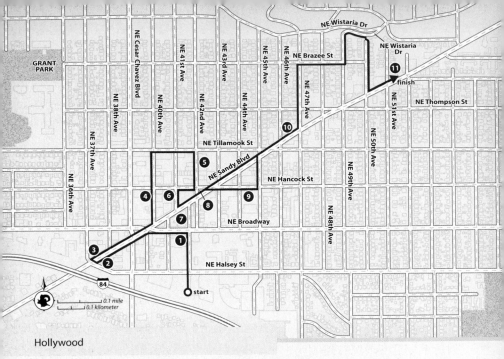

Hollywood

Points of Interest

1. **Chin's Kitchen** chinskitchenportland.com, 4126 NE Broadway St., 503-281-1203
2. **Wedge Head** wedgeheadpdx.com, 3728 NE Sandy Blvd., 503-477-7637
3. **Mountain Shop** mountainshop.net, 1510 NE 37th Ave., 503-288-6768
4. **Fleur de Lis** fleurdelisbakery.com, 3930 NE Hancock St., 503-459-4887
5. **The Moon and Sixpence** 2014 NE 42nd Ave., 503-288-7802
6. **Sam's Billiards** portlandpoolhall.com, 1845 NE 41st Ave., 503-282-8266
7. **Hollywood Theatre** hollywoodtheatre.org, 4122 NE Sandy Blvd., 503-493-1128
8. **Reo's Ribs** 4211 NE Sandy Blvd., 503-310-3600
9. **Hollywood Farmers Market** hollywoodfarmersmarket.org, NE Hancock St. between 44th and 45th Aves.
10. **Whole Bowl** thewholebowl.com, 4615 NE Sandy Blvd., 971-212-6154
11. **Laurelwood Public House** laurelwoodbrewpub.com, 5115 NE Sandy Blvd., 503-282-0622

20 Upper Sandy
Grotty to Grotto

Above: The Grotto, a 62-acre botanical garden surrounding a Catholic shrine

BOUNDARIES: NE 54th Ave., NE Sandy Blvd., NE Skidmore St.
DISTANCE: 2 miles
DIFFICULTY: Easy
PARKING: Free street parking, lot at The Grotto
PUBLIC TRANSIT: TriMet Bus 12 (NE Sandy Blvd. and 54th Ave., NE Sandy Blvd. and The Grotto)

Let's be up front about this: walking along Sandy Boulevard is unusual, unless you happen to work at one of a very limited number of occupations. It's not a street whose atmosphere is considered universally delightful. But it certainly has character, and it also has history. A lot of the things we'll point out on this walk don't exist anymore, but perhaps that's not so uncommon. The main thing to keep in mind is that Sandy Boulevard was invented for cars, in the age of automobile worship; in fact, it was so representative of this era that the Smithsonian Institution chose Sandy Boulevard for its permanent exhibit about automobile-oriented culture in the 1940s and

'50s, under the title *Suburban Strip*. (Yes, it also used to be considered suburban.) Walking up it, therefore, can be considered an exercise in shifting perspective. Relax and enjoy it.

Walk Description

We'll dive right in and start this walk at Northeast 55th Avenue and Sandy Boulevard, currently the location of ❶ **Clyde's Prime Rib.** Clyde's today is a fantastic old-school neighborhood steak-house, with curving, high-backed booths in the dining room, red-velvet seats in the bar, many gigantic fireplaces, and an actual suit of shining armor guarding the main entrance. There's live music in the lounge most nights, and until very recently, when he sold the place to another local restaurant runner, Clyde himself was often on hand, happily chatting with customers. But knowing the restaurant's uncomfortable history adds another layer to the experience: From the 1930s to the 1950s, it was a restaurant called the Coon Chicken Inn, a fried-chicken joint whose name and logo consisted of what today are shocking racist stereotypes. The place closed when the owners retired in the 1950s and the staff realized that times had changed. (There were two other restaurants in the chain, one in Seattle and one in Salt Lake City, which both also shut down during the 1950s.)

Half a block up Northeast Sandy Boulevard from Clyde's is the interestingly revamped ❷ **Fire Station 28,** which was built in 1913 as a barn and then renovated in 2005. The spiky, glowing sculpture in front of the building is called *Araminta: Carrying People to Safety,* by Portland artist James M. Harrison; its title refers to the abolitionist Harriet Tubman (Araminta is the name she was given at birth).

Continue up Sandy, stopping whenever the craving hits you at any of the great ethnic restaurants (mostly Thai and Vietnamese) along this stretch. Save room, though, for at least a couple of the truly excellent doughnuts at ❸ **Annie's,** just past Southeast 71st Avenue, where Sandy meets Northeast Fremont Street. Portland has any number of artisanal doughnut shops these days, with trendy flavors like lavender-blueberry or strawberry-basil, and we have no problem with that—but a classic is a classic. There's no atmosphere to speak of at Annie's, but you won't need it; the doughnuts take care of everything. Get an apple fritter—for starters.

Just across Fremont in a wedge-shaped building is ❹ **Fairley's Pharmacy,** which is cool not just for its geometrical architecture but also because it still has an old-fashioned soda fountain, with the counter and barstools and everything. Fairley's also appeared in Gus Van Sant's 1989 movie *Drugstore Cowboy.*

Speaking of movies, just across the street is the single-screen ❺ **Roseway Theater,** one of the best of many excellent places to see a first-run movie in Portland. It has a killer sound system and a huge screen, plus loads of retro charm and popcorn that everyone says is the best in all of Portland. (Research on this last topic is still being conducted, but I have no reason to doubt the claim.)

A couple of blocks up Sandy, you'll come to a funny-looking bottle-shaped building painted a disconcertingly murderous shade of red. This is (or was) the Sandy Jug, known these days as ❻ **Pirate's Cove,** and it's an example of the mimetic architecture that once made this street so much fun to cruise up and down. Basically, there used to be a lot of buildings on Sandy that were shaped like the thing they were selling. Originally built in 1928–29, the Jug has been an auto mechanic's shop, a café, a soda shop, a pool hall, and—for the past 15 years or so—a strip club. For years it was known both informally and officially as the Sandy Jug, but it seems to have embraced its new incarnation as Pirate's Cove with several nods to swashbuckler decor inside (and, it must be said, abundant booty).

Pirate's Cove makes for a nice contrast with our next stop; luckily, you'll have plenty of time to walk off the sleaze before we get there. Continue up Sandy Boulevard for several blocks (noting, on your left at Northeast 80th Avenue, the Park City Pub—this was once the steakhouse with the best name of any steakhouse ever: Sir Loins). Cross Northeast 82nd Avenue and continue a few more blocks until you see the entrance to ❼ **The Grotto** on your right (at about Northeast 85th Avenue). Go on in and follow signs to the visitors' entrance.

Officially called The National Sanctuary of Our Sorrowful Mother—you can see why the shorter moniker caught on—it's a 62-acre botanical garden surrounding a Catholic shrine. The actual grotto is a rock cave that was carved into the base of a hundred-foot cliff in 1923, with a replica of Michelangelo's *Pietà* nestled within it. Surrounding this are gardens on two levels, one of which is accessible by elevator as well as on foot (there's a fee for the lift, though). Wandering around the grounds of The Grotto is a possibly disorienting experience for anyone coming directly from a walk down Sandy Boulevard, but it's a quiet and calming pocket of nature and, if nothing else, a vivid juxtaposition. It's also a reliably cool retreat from the heat on a hot summer day, thanks to its position in a little hollow and its thick covering of trees.

To return to your starting point, simply cross to the other side of Sandy Boulevard outside the entrance to The Grotto; you can catch TriMet Bus 12 at Sandy and Northeast 68th Avenue.

Connecting the Walks

This route could be walked as a continuation of **Walk 19: Hollywood** (page 99)

Upper Sandy

Points of Interest

1. **Clyde's Prime Rib** clydesprimerib.com, 5474 NE Sandy Blvd., 503-281-9200
2. **Fire Station 28** 5540 NE Sandy Blvd.
3. **Annie's Donuts** 3449 NE 72nd Ave., 503-284-2752
4. **Fairley's Pharmacy** fairleyspharmacy.com, 7206 NE Sandy Blvd., 503-284-1159
5. **Roseway Theater** rosewaytheater.com, 7229 NE Sandy Blvd., 503-282-2898
6. **Pirate's Cove** piratescoveportland.com, 7417 NE Sandy Blvd., 503-287-8900
7. **The Grotto** thegrotto.org, NE 85th Ave. and Sandy Blvd., 503-254-7371

21 Fremont to Williams
Shifting Gears

Above: Pip's Original serves mini doughnuts and chai.

BOUNDARIES: N. Williams Ave., NE Skidmore St., NE Fremont St., NE 50th Ave.
DISTANCE: 3.5 miles
DIFFICULTY: Easy
PARKING: Free street parking
PUBLIC TRANSIT: TriMet Bus 44 (N. Williams Ave. and NE Skidmore St.) or Bus 24
   (NE Fremont St. and 57th Ave.)

This walk starts at a lovely cemetery on top of a hill, then makes its way down the hill through various little hubs of commercial activity, most of which have sprung up fairly recently. The walk concludes with a stretch of funky Williams Avenue, a major bicycle corridor busy with new commercial development that's been drawing some of the most talked-about buildings and businesses in town. (The nature of this development has been strongly influenced by the fact that there's so much bicycle traffic along here; the two things tend to feed each other. If you've been curious about the much-hyped Portland bike culture, the Williams Avenue corridor is a good place to get an up-close look at it.) For several years, this area has been in flux, and it looks set to remain that way: if you walk it now, try walking it again in six months—I bet you'll see big changes.

Walk Description

Start at the bus stop at Northeast Fremont Street and 57th Avenue, next to the extremely beautiful ❶ Rose City Cemetery (established in 1906). In the middle of the main cemetery is a separate, enclosed Japanese Cemetery. Go in for a look, or simply wander down Fremont alongside the quiet, atmospheric grounds.

At Northeast 52nd Avenue you'll reach a small cluster of eateries and coffee shops, including Stanich's, a longstanding Portland sports bar known for its enormous burgers. George and Gladys Stanich opened the joint in 1949. Gladys cooked, and George became known as The Philosopher of Fremont. The place closed after Thrillist named its burger the best in America, and its closure drew a follow-up wave of media scrutiny that was still going strong at press time. On the next block is another local favorite, ❷ Pip's Original, with bite-size doughnuts and chai. If it happens to be your birthday, you get a dozen of the mini doughnuts free!

Around Northeast 42nd Avenue and Fremont is the tiny hub of Beaumont Village, which is essentially just a small neighborhood market (in a building called the Swiss House—you'll recognize it) with a handful of shops and cafés.

Continue west along what is now mostly residential Fremont Street for several blocks. At the bottom of a long hill, by Northeast 15th Avenue, is another hub of commercial activity, centered around a Whole Foods grocery store. In the next block are two good pubs (the Free House and the County Cork) and a coffee shop—hard to go wrong.

Keep walking along Fremont until you reach Irving Park on your left, just past Northeast 11th Avenue. This hilly, shady park is a great place to wander around or to bust out any picnic supplies you may have collected at the grocery store a few blocks back. (The park is named after an ancient mariner, or, rather, a sea captain who had a land claim here in Portland's early days.)

Stay on Fremont Street for several more blocks, crossing Northeast Martin Luther King Jr. Boulevard at the traffic signal and continuing on. At North Williams Avenue, turn right. Williams is one of the major north–south thoroughfares for bicycle traffic (note the nice wide bike lanes along this street). Nearly 3,000 cyclists commute along this corridor daily. A block or so farther along, the building on the right, between Beech and Failing Streets on Williams, is currently home to some of the best-loved eateries and drinkeries in Portland, including ❸ Tasty n Sons restaurant. It's run by the same chef who established the deeply loved Toro Bravo. There's nearly always a huge line, so get here early if you're interested in a table, especially at brunch. If you missed the chance for an espresso earlier, there's a Ristretto Roasters location here.

This building, called The Hub (not to be confused with the nearby HUB brewpub, which we'll get to in a second), was conceived as a European-style marketplace and renovated as such in 2008; in addition to Tasty n Sons and several other small businesses, its tenants include a naturopathic veterinarian, a yoga studio, and a restaurant that serves mainly oysters. Call it gentrification if you will—that's pretty much what it is—but whatever, it's a lovely building, and frankly it's hard to imagine complaining over a bowl of Tasty n Sons' Burmese red-pork stew.

Across the street is another good eating and drinking place, and an early arrival to this neighborhood: the ❹ Fifth Quadrant pub. It's run by Lompoc Brewing, so it serves the familiar and well-loved Lompoc brews, but the food is a little more sophisticated here, and the room itself is all blonde wood and honeyed lighting. Next door there's a tasting room, the Sidebar, where you can sample specialty beers that aren't available anywhere else. This is also the place to pick up a keg or a few bottles to go.

Continuing along North Williams Avenue, you'll pass any number of shops, bars, and restaurants, and probably twice as many as there were at the time this was written—the neighborhood has definitely been discovered. Try anything that looks interesting! There's a bicycle-themed brewpub on the left, run by ❺ Hopworks Urban Brewery, with custom bike frames hung over the bar, a water-bottle filling station, and a range of organic microbrews on tap. The brewpub occupies the ground floor of an apartment building, called ecoFLATS, which is designed around sustainability, bike-friendliness, low energy use, and beer. (There's a flat-screen TV monitor in the entryway to the apartments that displays the amount of energy consumption for each tenant, in real time. Motivating!) The building's appearance is in line with several other new apartment blocks of recent vintage: sleek and square, with slightly weathered-looking and reclaimed materials whose rough textures provide an appealing contrast with the building's precise shapes and clean lines. It's a good look, although it's hard to say if the style will age well.

A little farther along, at the corner of North Williams and Northeast Skidmore Street, you'll find the very friendly and comfortable ❻ Vendetta, a totally unpretentious hangout of a bar with a large, covered patio and a pair of garage-style main doors that are kept open in warm weather. There's a shuffleboard table and usually really good local art on the walls. Overall the place has the settled, established feel of a beloved neighborhood spot that makes it a nice anchor for this rapidly growing, changing area.

Retrace your steps back to Northeast Fremont Street and catch Bus 24 heading east.

Fremont to Williams

Points of Interest

1 **Rose City Cemetery** 5625 NE Fremont St.

2 **Pip's Original**   4759 NE 42nd Ave., 503-206-8692

3 **Tasty n Sons** tastynsons.com, 3808 N. Williams Ave., 503-621-1400

4 **Fifth Quadrant** lompocbrewing.com, 3901 N. Williams Ave., 503-288-3996

5 **Hopworks Urban Brewery** hopworksbeer.com, 3947 N. Williams Ave., 503-287-6258

6 **Vendetta** vendettapdx.com, 4306 N. Williams Ave., 503-288-1085

22 Mississippi to Killingsworth
Upwardly Mobile

Above: Catch a show at Mississippi Studios and the adjacent Bar Bar.

BOUNDARIES: NE Killingsworth St., N. Mississippi Ave., N. Tillamook St., Martin Luther King Jr. Blvd.
DISTANCE: 2 miles
DIFFICULTY: Moderate
PARKING: Free street parking
PUBLIC TRANSIT: TriMet Bus 6 (NE Martin Luther King Jr. Blvd. and NE Killingsworth St.),
   MAX Yellow Line (Albina/Mississippi Station)

The Mississippi neighborhood is one of the more recently reinvigorated (or gentrified, if you must) parts of town. Walking through it still brings the excitement of discovery, and though it's not exactly rough around the edges anymore, it nevertheless preserves its past, often in the form of lovingly restored buildings with wholly new functions. With this walk, we follow North Mississippi Avenue from end to end and then join up with North Killingsworth Street, one of Northeast Portland's main thoroughfares.

Walk Description

Start at the Albina/Mississippi MAX Station. From here, turn right onto North Mississippi Avenue. One block up, North Russell Street is worth a one-block side trip in either direction: to the left you'll find ❶ **Widmer Brothers Brewing Company,** one of Portland's pioneering brewpubs, housed in a former theater building; to the right (uphill) is one of the local McMenamin Brothers' more agreeable properties, the ❷ **White Eagle.** Once upon a time, the White Eagle was a fairly disreputable hotel and rowdy dock-worker drinking establishment, nicknamed the Bucket of Blood for its frequent and messy bar brawls. These days it's a perfectly civilized bar-restaurant with live country-folk music most nights. It's supposed to be haunted, so stay alert. (There are also hotel rooms upstairs, if you're thinking of staying awhile.)

But don't get sidetracked for too long; we're just getting started. Continue straight ahead along North Mississippi Avenue, following the S-curve of the road as it passes beneath the I-5 and I-405 overpasses. It's a fairly steep climb to the top of the hill, but the path flattens out just past North Fremont Street. (As you climb, note on your right the Ecliptic Brewing building, where you can taste some of the best and most astronomically named beer in the city, along with some very good food.)

The Meadow, specializing in gourmet salts, is one of several shops on Mississippi.

Halfway down the block on your left is ❸ **The ReBuilding Center,** a cool idea in a cool space: it's a nonprofit that gathers used building materials (from demolitions, donations, and the like) that might otherwise have been thrown out, then sells them as part of a sustainable-building effort. Far from the cookie-cutter stuff you might find at an ordinary retail store, the fixtures, frames, and various odds and ends here are unique enough that it's fun just to browse. There's an "idea library" for those seeking inspiration. And the building itself embodies the principles in which it trades: it's a funky hodgepodge of salvaged material that somehow looks just right when put together.

At the corner of North Beech Street and Mississippi Avenue, on the right, is one of the more appealing brewpubs in town, ④ **StormBreaker Brewing.** Its patio makes a great place to sit with a pint of kolsch and a pimento burger and watch the traffic go by. (The brewing company also has a new branch at 8409 N. Lombard St. in St. Johns, which you can visit on Walk 25, page 126.)

Diagonally across the street from StormBreaker Brewing is ⑤ **Bridge City Comics,** a fine, friendly, and completely unintimidating comic-book shop, known for the well-attended author events and readings it hosts. For more reading material, head to independent bookstore Another Read Through across the street on the next block.

As you continue along North Mississippi, note ⑥ **Sunlan Lighting** on your left, at North Failing Street. The shop itself is only mildly odd, but the commercials it used to run on late-night TV were of such a particular degree of bizarre that any local who has lived here long enough to have seen them will know exactly what you're talking about when asked. (Incidentally, it's a great place to find lightbulbs in unusual sizes, should you need any.)

A few doors down is ⑦ **Mississippi Studios,** a small live-music venue, and its attached watering hole, called ⑦ **Bar Bar.** The venue is intimate and impeccably booked, with a sort of tiny-screening-room feel plus a balcony, and the bar serves awesome burgers that start at just $7. Alert walkers may also notice that the bar's outdoor patio makes use of materials from The ReBuilding Center down the street. This is definitely one of the best places to see a band (or just hang out and grab a bite), but get there early, because it does fill up.

Farther along North Mississippi is ⑧ **Paxton Gate,** a store that is almost more of a taxidermy museum. (The original location, in San Francisco, started out as a gardening store, but it took off in an unexpected direction fairly soon.) It bills itself as a shop for "Treasures and Oddities," a place to find things for your personal wonder cabinet: fossils, bones, teeth, and eyes; adorable terrariums; etchings; mysterious items in jars; and, of course, the odd gardening implement. Definitely worth a look around, and the interior of the store itself is beautiful too.

At North Prescott Street, Mississippi kinks to the right and becomes North Albina Avenue. Make your way along Albina for several blocks until you reach North Killingsworth Street; turn right on Killingsworth.

A few blocks east along Killingsworth is the ⑨ **North Portland** branch of the county library—originally the Carnegie Library, built in 1913. It was restored in 1999 and looks fantastic inside and out. Across the street, just past North Commercial Avenue on Killingsworth, is a very turquoise dive bar called ⑩ **The Florida Room,** famous for its Bloody Marys.

Back on the other side of Killingsworth Street is the ⑪ **Chapel Pub,** a cute little building originally from 1932, now yet another in the string of drinkeries in repurposed buildings owned by the local McMenamins chain.

At the corner of Northeast Killingsworth Street and North Williams Avenue you'll find the location of the now sadly closed In Other Words, a volunteer-run feminist bookstore and community center that was skewered on *Portlandia* and eventually cut ties with the show (via a strongly worded blog post and sign in the window), saying the show had a "net negative effect" on the neighborhood and the city as a whole.

If you'd like to test the truth of that view or you just have some energy to burn, retrace your steps and head back (west) along Killingsworth to explore the many eating and drinking options in that direction. If not, hop the   at North Interstate Avenue, or retrace your steps to North Albina Avenue and catch Bus 4 back toward the city center and your starting point.

The Florida Room is famous for its Bloody Marys.

Mississippi to Killingsworth

Points of Interest

1 Widmer Brothers Brewing Company widmerbrothers.com/brewery, 929 N. Russell St., 503-281-2437

2 White Eagle mcmenamins.com/whiteeaglesaloon, 836 N. Russell St., 503-282-6810

3 The ReBuilding Center rebuildingcenter.org, 3625 N. Mississippi Ave., 503-331-1877

4 StormBreaker Brewing stormbreakerbrewing, 832 N. Beech St., 971-703-4516

5 Bridge City Comics bridgecitycomics.com, 3725 N. Mississippi Ave., 503-282-5484

6 Sunlan Lighting sunlanlighting.com, 3901 N. Mississippi Ave., 503-281-0453

7 Mississippi Studios and Bar Bar mississippistudios.com, 3939 N. Mississippi Ave., 503-288-3895

8 Paxton Gate paxtongatepdx.com, 4204 N. Mississippi Ave., 503-719-4508

9 North Portland Library multcolib.org, 512 N. Killingsworth St., 503-988-5394

10 The Florida Room floridaroom.org, 435 N. Killingsworth St., 503-287-5658

11 Chapel Pub mcmenamins.com/chapel, 430 N. Killingsworth St., 503-286-0372

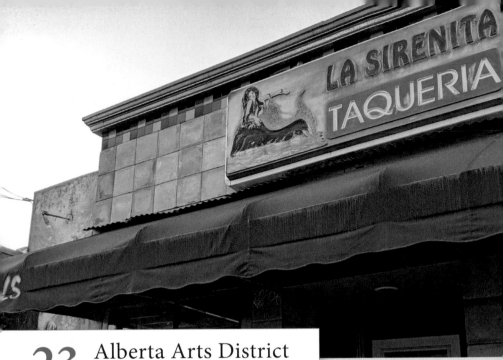

23 Alberta Arts District
Artisan Living

Above: La Sirenita was one of Portland's first hipster Mexican restaurants.

BOUNDARIES: NE 33rd Ave., NE Ninth Ave., NE Alberta St.
DISTANCE: 1.25 miles
DIFFICULTY: Easy
PARKING: Free street parking
PUBLIC TRANSIT: TriMet Bus 72 (NE Alberta St. and Ninth Ave.), Bus 70 (NE Alberta St. and 33rd Ave.)

If you'd left Portland in the early 1990s and not heard a word about it since, you would be astounded by the changes that have since taken place along Northeast Alberta Street. Back then, more than half of the businesses were shuttered, and nobody yet was using the term *gentrification* anywhere near here. But things change quickly. As is ever the way, bold artistic types noticed the cheap rent and made their way over, hipsters and hangers-on soon followed, and then came the business dollars, the building renovations, the local press's guilt-ridden griping about forcing longtime locals out of the neighborhood, followed by still more emboldened newcomers . . . you know the story.

These days the district has settled into its comfortably gentrified role; the identity crises seem mostly to have passed. It's now considered one of the most desirable neighborhoods in Portland, and it boasts a thriving arts scene that has matured significantly since its early days of silly post-hippie summer-camp crafting displays. The last Thursday of each month, Alberta turns into a chaotic street fair that has only nominally to do with artists and art galleries. Thousands of people attend—don't plan on driving or parking anywhere near here on those evenings. It's well worth seeing, though, even if it's not necessarily everyone's cup of tea. If street fairs aren't your thing, don't despair: this part of town easily holds its own any day of the week.

Walk Description

Start at the bus stop at Northeast Alberta Street and Ninth Avenue. From here you can see the landmark French Gothic towers of ❶ St. Andrew Catholic Church. This spot has been home to a chapel since 1907, when a group of Irish immigrants pooled their resources to buy the land. It's known today as a diverse and open-minded organization, reflecting the character of the neighborhood.

Head east on Northeast Alberta. Wander up a block or so until you reach Northeast 10th Avenue, where on your left you'll see ❷ The Bye and Bye, a great bar and restaurant with awesome mason-jar drinks and a menu of Southern comfort food that just happens to be entirely vegan. The space is beautiful, and the crowd tends to be as well.

At Northeast 16th Avenue is ❸ Green Bean Books, an excellent children's bookstore the likes of which every kid ought to have the chance to explore at some point. There are all kinds of nooks and crannies to cozy up in, plus fun little gifts, a summertime garden and deck, and regular events, including author readings, crafts nights, and multilingual story time sessions.

Continue up the street until you reach about Northeast 20th Avenue, at which point you'll begin to smell the heavenly sweetness that is ❹ Salt & Straw. This artisan-ice-cream shop (which started out as a tiny mobile cart, like many other successful Portland food ventures) has quickly become an obsession for locals and tourists alike; it now has three locations in Portland, as well as several others in California and Seattle. You can even get it shipped to your house. People stand in line for ages to get their hands on a scoop or two of the salted caramel, or the balsamic strawberry, or the honey lavender. At first glance this seems ridiculous, lining up around the block to wait for ice cream, until you taste the stuff. OK, even then it's a little bit ridiculous, but I dare you to try walking blithely past the front door once you catch a whiff of this place.

At Northeast 27th Avenue, duck around the corner to the left to find ❺ Monograph Bookwerks, a fine-art bookstore owned by a couple of artists (one of whom used to manage the sadly departed live music club LaLuna, among other notable credits). The shop sells rare and small-press art books, plus a carefully chosen selection of prints, objects, and supplies.

Across Northeast 27th Avenue from the bookshop you'll see the revamped Northwestern Electric Company Alberta Substation building, constructed in 1931 and now (after drastic renovations) a neighborhood pub called ❻ The Station. It's worth looking inside to see reminders of the building's former life in various photos, decor, and light fixtures.

Continuing along Alberta, just beyond Northeast 28th Avenue you'll come to ❼ La Sirenita, which for a very long time was pretty much the only place to get a decent taco or burrito within the city limits. These days the options are practically unlimited, but La Sirenita gets props for being here first.

A movie house from 1927 until 1978, the ❽ Alberta Rose Theatre at Northeast 30th Avenue was closed for 20 years until it reemerged as a 300-seat live-music venue. It's also home to a variety of spoken-word performances, talks, and lectures, including the *Mortified* series and *Science on Tap*, a program of entertaining, beer-fueled discussions of various timely issues and phenomena in the scientific world.

Opened in 1999, ❾ Vita Cafe was part of the vanguard of both the Alberta restaurant scene and the wave of vegan-vegetarian dining options in Portland. This was in the era before anyone had given much thought to gluten, pro or con, and tofu was generally considered a form of punishment. The Vita dedicated itself to using sustainable business practices and became a leader in thoughtful restaurant dining, all the while churning out meals that made healthy eating taste good. The staff worked with locally and organically produced ingredients, and the restaurant dedicated a percentage of sales to environmental nonprofits. Some people might have found these practices a little stuffy at the time, or at least intimidatingly pure-hearted, but these days it just seems like ordinary good behavior. Progress!

Northeast Alberta Street is so densely packed with things to look at that the best way to return to the starting point is simply to retrace your steps. If you're tired, though, you can also catch Bus 72.

Alberta Arts District

Points of Interest

1. St. Andrew Catholic Church standrewchurch.com, 806 NE Alberta St., 503-281-4429
2. The Bye and Bye thebyeandbye.com, 1011 NE Alberta St., 503-281-0537
3. Green Bean Books greenbeanbookspdx.com, 1600 NE Alberta St., 503-954-2354
4. Salt & Straw saltandstraw.com, 2035 NE Alberta St., 503-208-3867
5. Monograph Bookwerks monographbookwerks.com, 5005 NE 27th Ave., 503-284-5005
6. The Station stationpdx.com, 2703 NE Alberta St., 503-284-4491
7. La Sirenita 2817 NE Alberta St., 503-335-8283
8. Alberta Rose Theatre albertarosetheatre.com, 3000 NE Alberta St., 503-719-6055
9. Vita Cafe vita-cafe.com, 3023 NE Alberta St., 503-335-8233

24 Historic Kenton
Paul Bunyan Territory

Above: Have coffee and peruse local art at Posies Bakery & Cafe.

BOUNDARIES: N. Columbia Blvd., I-5, N. Chautauqua Blvd., N. Lombard St.
DISTANCE: 1 mile
DIFFICULTY: Easy
PARKING: Free street parking
PUBLIC TRANSIT: TriMet MAX Yellow Line (Kenton/N. Denver Station)

Historic Kenton is a funky little out-of-the-way part of town that has a no-nonsense, totally unpretentious center and an interesting past. Kenton began as a company town in 1911, founded by the Swift Meat Packing Company. These days it might be best known as having been the home of former Portland Mayor Sam Adams or for its charmingly named strip club, the Dancin' Bare. The area has benefited recently from a $2.85 million "greenscaping" and revitalization program courtesy of the Portland Development Commission and the city's Bureau of Transportation. New businesses and shopfronts have been moving in, and young barflies have been known to travel from the depths of Southeast Portland to see indie bands play at Kenton watering holes. Plus it has its own branch of the Portland Farmers Market on Wednesday afternoons June–September (at North Denver Avenue and McClellan Street), as well as a rollicking annual street fair each spring. Kenton's most famous landmark (despite the charming bravado of The World Famous Kenton Club) is the giant Paul Bunyan statue at the intersection of North Interstate and Denver Avenues, near the MAX station; it's a relic from the Oregon Centennial celebrations in Kenton in 1959.

Walk Description

Start at the Kenton/North Denver MAX Station. Across the street is the giant Paul Bunyan lumberjack statue. He's 35 feet tall and was put here in 1959 to welcome folks who came to Portland for the Oregon Centennial Exposition, but now he serves primarily to set an example for fashion trends among the young men of the Portland area. (Just kidding. Mostly.) Head south along North Denver Avenue past the historic Kenton Hotel, home to the tiny 7 Bucks a Wack barbershop and ❷ **Kenton Station,** a friendly neighborhood pub with a good breakfast. On the opposite side of the street, you'll pass the ❸ **Tavern on Denver,** known locally for having the coldest beers around—useful information if you happen to be walking here on a hot August afternoon. Half a block farther is ❹ **Posies Bakery & Cafe,** where you should definitely have a scone or a sandwich. This is a tiny, lovely, locally owned, kid-friendly community hangout with great coffee and baked treats, and rotating displays of artwork on the walls. The café is part of the monthly Third Thursday Art Walk in Kenton.

Take a quick detour to the left on North Kilpatrick Street to the (deservedly, although not actually) ❺ **World Famous Kenton Club,** an excellent lowbrow hangout with a rocky facade; a truly elaborate wood-paneled interior; cheap drinks; fried food; live music; and a friendly, rowdy crowd. The bar adopted the *famous* part of its name after it appeared briefly in the 1971 movie *Kansas City Bomber,* in which actress and sex symbol Raquel Welch plays a scrappy roller derby girl. (Posters from the movie hang inside the bar near the stage.)

Retrace your steps back to Denver Avenue, taking note of ❻ **Po'Shines Café De La Soul,** a welcoming soul-food restaurant on the corner; it's run by a pastor and has a catering arm that offers culinary and life-skills training to at-risk youth and adults. If it's open and you haven't eaten, I recommend stopping in for a bite. Then continue another block or so along North Denver Avenue and you'll come to ❼ **Kenton Antiques.** A labor of love run by a woman who left the corporate world to buy the place a few years ago, the store offers all kinds of goodies, from nice vintage furniture to Pez dispensers.

At North Schofield Street take a right. On the next corner is the Historic Kenton Firehouse, home to the **8** **North Portland Tool Library.** The tool library does just what you'd imagine: it lends tools, free of charge, to neighborhood residents who need to use them but might not want (or be able) to buy their own. (Seriously, how often are you really going to use a belt sander? Wouldn't it make more sense just to borrow one?) It also holds regular hands-on workshops (free of charge) so people can learn how to use the tools they're borrowing.

Follow North Schofield Street until you get to North Delaware Avenue, and turn right. Veer right again, just before North Halleck Street, to enter **9** **Kenton Park.** You can either make a loop around the edges of the park or take the paved pathway that steers you diagonally through the center. On a hot day, seek out the "spraypark," which takes running through the sprinklers to a whole new level.

At the far (northeast) corner of the park, you'll come to North Argyle Street; turn right. On the right is **1** **Salvage Works,** which has all kinds of vintage building materials and various odds and ends. After plenty of browsing and daydreaming about giving your home (or imaginary home) a makeover, veer right at North Interstate Avenue to return to the starting point and good old Paul Bunyan.

Connecting the Walks

The starting point of this walk makes for an easy connection with **Walk 26: Columbia River Walk** (page 130).

A ball field is just one of the amenities at Kenton Park.

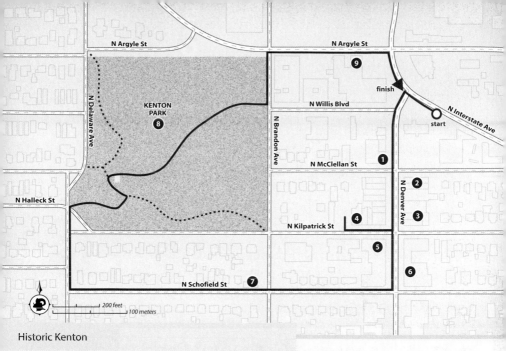

Historic Kenton

Points of Interest

1 **Salvage Works** salvageworkspdx.com, 2030 N. Willis Blvd., 503-285-2555

2 **Kenton Station** kentonstationportland.com, 8303 N. Denver Ave., 503-286-9242

3 **Tavern on Denver** 8234 N. Denver Ave., 503-285-7010

4 **Posies Bakery & Cafe** posiescafe.com, 8208 N. Denver Ave., 503-289-1319

5 **The World Famous Kenton Club** kentonclub.com, 2025 N. Kilpatrick St., 503-285-3718

6 **Po'Shines Café De La Soul** 8139 N. Denver Ave., 503-978-9000

7 **Kenton Antiques** kentonantiquespdx.com, 8112 N. Denver Ave., 503-490-8855

8 **North Portland Tool Library** northportlandtoollibrary.org, 2209 N. Schofield St., 503-823-0209

9 **Kenton Park** portlandoregon.gov, 8417 N. Brandon Ave.

25 St. Johns and Cathedral Park
Far Away, So Close

Above: Signal Station Pizza was formerly an Art Deco gas station.

BOUNDARIES: N. Smith St., N. New York Ave., N. Ida Ave., Willamette River
DISTANCE: 2 miles
DIFFICULTY: Moderate (one steep hill)
PARKING: Free street parking (with time limits), lot at Cathedral Park
PUBLIC TRANSIT: TriMet Bus 75 (N. Lombard St. and Oswego Ave.) or Buses 11 and 16
   (N. Ivanhoe St. and Baltimore Ave.)

Lots of Portlanders have close friends they claim they never see anymore because the friends bought houses in St. Johns and it's *soooo* far away. And there may be something to that: though it has many charms, this little neighborhood is not exactly handy. It's about 9 miles and a 15- to 20-minute drive from downtown Portland, a little farther if you're coming from Southeast. But there was a crucial period when homes were comparatively affordable here, just as they were beginning to be priced out of reach for many people in Portland proper—and that just happened to be around the same time that Portland's too-cool, bored-with-it-all crowd began to discover that St. Johns had a huge amount of off-kilter charm (and a disproportionately high number of great and terrible bars for its size). St. Johns also has one of the area's most appealing parks, with easy access to the Willamette River and the prettiest bridge in Portland, hands-down. Come for the post-work swimming; stay for the sunset photo ops.

The saint in question, if you're curious, is James John, an early California import; he claimed a patch of land in 1843 and started platting the town.

Walk Description

Start at the bus stop at North Lombard Street and Oswego Avenue. Walk along Lombard toward town (west). Bear left on North Richmond Street, then turn right on North Ivanhoe Street.

At the corner of Richmond and Ivanhoe is the ❶ **St. Johns Theater & Pub,** where you can watch second-run movies in a quirkily charming atmosphere. Built in 1905 for the Lewis and Clark Expo, the pub was actually intended as a movie theater from the start, although it wasn't in St. Johns at the time. A church had it transported here by barge along the Willamette River after the exposition; in fact, it served as a church more than once in its history, and as an American Legion hall, before becoming a pub in 1989. It's now owned by the McMenamins, part of their mini-chain of microbrew theater pubs. The dome you see is not the original, but it's still very cute, and the inside has loads of character (plus beer, pizza, and movies—you really can't go wrong).

Take North Ivanhoe Street to North Charleston Avenue and turn right. Check out ❷ **Signal Station Pizza,** an old Art Deco gas station converted into a pizzeria. Hang a left onto North Lombard Street.

Continue along Lombard through what is essentially the main business strip of St. Johns. Stroll slowly and do a little window-shopping as you go. You'll also find a number of good spots for a bite; I'm partial to ❸ **Slim's** for good burgers and salads. It's also probably the best and most reliable option for nightlife in St. Johns, with a good range of beers, a friendly vibe, and live music in the evenings. (There's also the Fixin' To, a block east of Signal Station Pizza, with a cool patio, a good tap list, and a solid roster of indie bands playing live music several nights a week, but unless you're a fashionably bearded faux lumberjack or an American Apparel model, it's almost too hip to be fun.)

At North Burlington Avenue, turn right. Cross North Central Street and head into St. Johns Park. Make a loop around the park, then cross back over Central and onto North Chicago Avenue. When you get to North Lombard Street, turn left. A block farther is ❹ **The Wishing Well,** a combination Chinese restaurant and dive bar in an excellent (if rapidly decaying) building, with a cool sign to boot. Early hipsters making pilgrimages to St. Johns tried their best to make the Wishing Well bar a cool hangout, but it's just rough enough around the edges to have resisted all such efforts and remains a strictly no-frills watering hole.

Turn right on North Alta Avenue, then left on North Ivanhoe Street. At North Philadelphia Avenue turn right. The redbrick building across the street was originally City Hall, built in 1905. It's now occupied by a training division of the Portland Police.

At North Syracuse Street take a right to get back onto North Alta Avenue, onto which you'll turn left and walk a block before turning right on North Willamette Boulevard, then left on North Baltimore Avenue to head down a steep hill toward the river.

Just past North Decatur Street stands a big orange industrial-looking building. In its court-yard you'll find, among a handful of other businesses, ❺ Occidental Brewing Co., a scrappy little microbrewery with excellent beers you can try either in the taproom in the corner of its factory space or in the next-door *Wursthaus* with a rooftop view of the St. Johns Bridge (along with a nice menu of mostly German food specialties). The kolsch was its signature brew for years, but these days Occidental's range of beers has expanded to around 10 styles, including the tasty fall seasonal Festbier. It's well worth stopping in; you can also get a growler of beer to take with you.

Beyond the brewery, cross the railroad tracks and go straight to enter Cathedral Park. This is one of the nicest parks in Portland, partly because of its awesome view of the St. Johns Bridge, whose 40-story-tall Gothic cathedral spires and slender silhouette look good from pretty much any angle. The St. Johns Bridge was built in 1931 by David B. Steinman, who built an awful lot of bridges in his time but claimed this one as his favorite. As for the park, it was recognized as a good hangout early on: Lewis and Clark apparently stopped here, camping overnight, in 1806. It was also the landing point for the ferry between St. Johns and Linnton, across the river (one of neighborhood founder James John's projects). But it didn't officially become a park until 1980. These days it's the site of an annual jazz festival and several other events.

It's an appreciably steep climb back up the hill to the starting point. Walk up North Baltimore Avenue until you reach North Lombard Street, where you can either catch Bus 44 or turn right and walk back to North Oswego Avenue, where we began.

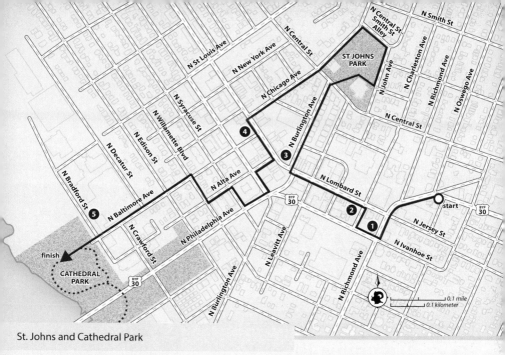

St. Johns and Cathedral Park

Points of Interest

1. St. Johns Theater & Pub mcmenamins.com/stjohns, 8203 N. Ivanhoe St., 503-283-8520
2. Signal Station Pizza signalstationpizza.com, 8302 N. Lombard St., 503-286-2257
3. Slim's Restaurant & Lounge 8635 N. Lombard St, 503-286-3854
4. The Wishing Well wishingwellportland.com, 8800 N. Lombard St., 503-286-4434
5. Occidental Brewing Co. occidentalbrewing.com, 6635 N. Baltimore Ave., 503-719-7102

26 Columbia River Walk
Desolation Row

Above: Watch river traffic from the bicycle-and-foot path along Marine Drive.

BOUNDARIES: N. Marine Dr., N. Portland Rd., Columbia Slough, I-5
DISTANCE: 5 miles
DIFFICULTY: Easy
PARKING: Free street parking
PUBLIC TRANSIT: TriMet Interstate MAX Yellow Line (Kenton/N. Denver Ave., Expo Center Stations)

If you read much in the way of nature writing or all those soothingly contemplative travelogues about long-distance cross-country walking, sooner or later you'll come across a mention of so-called ghost roads or ghost trails. The expression can mean a few different things, depending on the context and the speaker. Some ghost trails are old walking paths that still exist on maps but have mostly faded from the earth, due to lack of maintenance or a newer, better alternative. Others may have started as deer trails that never made it onto a map and aren't officially maintained but can still be very useful, if you have the skills and inclination to spot them. In parts of medieval Europe, ghost roads were the ones that led to and from cemeteries.

This walk isn't really any of those things, but I wouldn't be surprised if somewhere along the route you should happen to see a ghost. We won't be visiting any medieval graveyards, but here's the thing: in certain weather or a certain mood, you might begin to feel just a little bit of desolation on this walk. You might wonder if maybe it's a little bit haunted.

Most of the time, though, this is simply a great-wide-open, middle-of-nowhere, get-out-and-stretch-your-legs walk. Though it passes by several heavy-industry areas, with all the accompanying toxic leftovers, it also incorporates some of the more interesting natural features of the Portland region and the site of a historic residential development that was needlessly destroyed in a flood. In short, this walk provides plenty of opportunity to meditate on things that have vanished without a trace, as well as the things we leave behind that can never be completely erased.

There's not a lot in the way of refreshments or entertainment out here, so bring whatever supplies you might need, and prepare to cover a bit of ground.

Walk Description

Start at the Kenton/North Denver Avenue MAX Station. Take a moment to marvel at the statue of Paul Bunyan on the far side of the MAX tracks. (For more about him, see Walk 24: Historic Kenton, page 122.) Staying on the north side of the tracks, take the sidewalk past ❶ George's Dancin' Bare—bet you can't guess what that is—and cross North Argyle Street. Cross the MAX tracks and continue onto the pedestrian strip along the North Interstate Avenue overpass.

Follow North Interstate across the Columbia Slough (it rhymes with *blue*). Then cross at the traffic light where Interstate meets North Schmeer Road, and hang a right onto the pedestrian-only Columbia Slough Trail.

As you make your way along the Columbia Slough Trail, you might see (or, more likely, hear) off to your right the ❷ Portland International Raceway, where the Oregon Motorcycle Road Racing Association (omrra.com) holds competitive events throughout the summer; there are also weekly drag races and motocross competitions, trade shows, "drifting" demos, and all manner of gearhead entertainment. If there's a race on when you're in the area, it's well worth going to see. (Better yet, volunteer as a corner worker during one of OMRRA's events in exchange for which you get free admission, free lunch, eternal gratitude, and the best view of the races. Details about volunteering are on OMRRA's website, along with a schedule. There's a constant need for volunteers, and anybody can do it; all it takes is showing up the morning of the event.)

The body of water you're walking alongside, the Columbia Slough, is part of a complicated wetlands system making up a 60-mile watershed in North Portland. The slough runs just south of the Smith and Bybee Wetlands (worth a visit, if you have extra time) and parallels the Columbia River for 18 miles until the Columbia's confluence with the Willamette River near Kelley Point Park (also a nice place to wander around, dip your toes in the water, and have a picnic, if you're in the area).

The slough has a reputation for being polluted, due partly to its decades of being surrounded by heavy industry (not to mention general drainage from Portland), some of which historically has consisted of combined sewer overflow during periods of heavy rain. Which might at first sound off-putting, but don't worry—the slough is perfectly safe to use as a recreational zone (for kayaking, hiking, birding, wildlife-spotting, etc.) and continues to serve its original function as part of the city's flood-control system. If you have access to a kayak or canoe, the slough is one of several urban waterways in Portland that make for a fun and rewarding paddle. But it's also well worth exploring on foot. If you'd like to extend this walk, you can stay on the trail that parallels the full length of the slough in either direction.

Follow the Columbia Slough Trail until you see the railroad bridge at North Portland Road. Turn right onto the walking path alongside North Portland, and follow it through a wild, remote industrial zone. On your left is Smith Lake, part of the ❸ **Smith and Bybee Wetlands Natural Area,** notable for being the largest protected wetlands area within a city in the United States. On your right are Heron Lakes Golf Course and the former site of Vanport City.

During the 1940s, Vanport was the largest wartime housing development in the country. Defense workers rushing to Portland, mostly in shipbuilding, needed a place to live, so in 1942 a 650-acre parcel of the Columbia River floodplain was turned into a massive housing project. More than 9,000 apartments were built on the swampy land; with more than 40,000 residents at its peak, Vanport was the second-largest city in Oregon. It was also racially segregated and generally discontented; the Housing Authority of Portland at the time called it "troublesome" and "blighted."

After the war ended, most of the people who stayed on in Vanport were African Americans. On Memorial Day in 1948, the Columbia River overflowed its floodplain. Residents of Vanport had all of 35 minutes to escape. The hastily built wooden apartments washed away in moments; within hours, nothing was left. At least 15 people died. Rumors lingered that authorities had purposely neglected to warn Vanport residents until the last minute. In any case, those who'd been flooded out of their homes suddenly had nowhere to live; many of them settled in North and Northeast Portland, establishing what was to become the heart of Portland's black community.

At the river, cross North Marine Drive and turn right. (The land you see across the water is Hayden Island, home to the Jantzen Beach shopping area and, to the west, a lot of undeveloped land. The Port of Portland briefly planned to annex West Hayden Island for industrial use, but plans were dropped.) You are now walking parallel to the Oregon section of the Columbia River (the Washington state line is on the other side of Hayden Island). Follow the trail along the water's edge until it curves back in toward North Marine Drive (also known as North Swift Highway and OR 120).

Follow along parallel with North Marine Drive past the Expo Center's huge parking lot, where you'll come to a large four-way intersection. Here, cross Marine Drive, then turn right (heading back in the direction you came from) about 100 meters until you see on your left the walkway to the Portland Expo Center MAX Station. (There's a #11 bus stop here too.) Follow this curved path to the station, where the Yellow Line will take you back into town.

Connecting the Walks

This walk's starting point makes for an easy connection with **Walk 24: Historic Kenton** (page 122).

Learn more about the flooded city of Vanport on the Columbia Slough Trail.

Columbia River Walk

Points of Interest

1 George's Dancin' Bare georgesdancinbare.com, 8440 N. Interstate Ave., 503-285-9073

2 Portland International Raceway portlandraceway.com, 1940 N. Victory Blvd., 503-823-7223

3 Smith and Bybee Wetlands Natural Area oregonmetro.gov, 5300 N. Marine Dr., 503-797-1545

27 Lents
A Town Cut in Two

Above: The Eagle Eye Tavern is a neighborhood hangout with pinball and pool tables.

BOUNDARIES: SE 92nd Ave., SE Holgate Blvd., SE 72nd Ave., SE Woodstock Blvd.
DISTANCE: 1.5 miles
DIFFICULTY: Easy
PARKING: Free street parking
PUBLIC TRANSIT: MAX Green Line (SE Holgate Blvd. and Lents/SE Foster Stations); you could also get here via the I-205 multiuse path

The actual neighborhood of Lents—named after Oliver Perry Lent, a pioneer who ran a 190-acre farm in the area in 1866—is fairly large (nearly 4 square miles), but its downtown core is barely there. With all the boarded-up shopfronts and papered-over windows, it has an almost ghost-town appeal. This is mainly because Lents got the short end of the transit stick back when Portland was trying to figure out where the I-205 freeway should go. (It had been planned for 39th Avenue, but folks in the powerful and moneyed Laurelhurst neighborhood wouldn't have it.)

By running the freeway along Southeast 95th Avenue, city leaders basically cut the historic core of Lents in half, leaving it more a traffic hub than anything else. Still, it's the center of one of the largest and most diverse parts of Portland, with more Asian, Latino, and Russian immigrants than most other parts of town. In 1998 it was named an Urban Renewal Area, which allows the city to use property-tax funds for improvement projects. A striking number of shiny new mixed-use and apartment buildings, including a decent amount of affordable housing, have been popping up near the town center in recent years. The Lents neighborhood park is one of the nicest in the Portland area. And the weekly farmers market here draws folks from much closer in, thanks to its ethnically diverse makeup and resulting tendency to offer produce you can't find at other markets. Things might be looking up for Lents . . . eventually.

Walk Description

Start the walk at the Southeast Holgate Boulevard MAX Station, on the Green Line. From the station, cross Holgate and head right (west) until you reach Southeast 92nd Avenue, where you'll enter Lents Park.

The park (like the neighborhood) is named for stonemason Oliver Lent, who had a land claim here in the 1850s. (It was his son who laid out the town plan in the 1890s; not yet part of Portland, it was called the town of Lent). Locals have been gathering up land to use as park space since the 1940s, and the city established an official plan for its layout in 1953. The park includes a good-sized stadium ringed with trees, plus a couple of smaller softball fields, two soccer fields, tennis courts, a playground and bouldering area, and footpaths linking them all. At the southern end, picnic tables are arranged beneath beautiful old-growth trees.

Wander the length of Lents Park along the footpaths until you reach its southern boundary, at Southeast Steele Street; turn left to get back to Southeast 92nd Avenue. At 92nd, turn right and walk several blocks toward the Lents town center, such as it is.

Once upon a time (in the 1890s), streetcars used to run through here, connecting Lents with downtown Portland (via the Hawthorne Bridge) and linking up with the Interurban Trolley that went to Gresham and Estacada. Portland annexed the original town of Lent in 1912, during a time when it was basically annexing any and every little settlement within a reasonable distance. But as it turned out, annexation didn't do Lents any favors; the city continued to neglect this far-flung neighborhood, and scant resources came its way in terms of transport and infrastructure improvements. Then came the insult of the I-205 construction. That trend continued for, well, most of Lents's history, until about the late 1990s. At the corner of Southeast 92nd Avenue and

Harold Street, you'll see a wide-open field that is the temporary home of the beloved ❶ Belmont Goats. The herd of 14 goats and their pet hen, Juniper, have become a legitimate tourist attraction, a little slice of rural farm life in the midst of the city. They're taken care of by a staff of volunteers; the herd originally lived in a grass lot on Southeast Belmont Street but moved here a few years ago, and staff are now on the lookout for their next home. Wherever they end up, it's fun to hang out and watch them play; they seem to have an ability to work their magic on anyone's mood. (It's impossible not to be cheerful while watching a herd of goats play.)

A little farther along Southeast 92nd Avenue is the site of the ❷ Lents International Farmers Market (June–October, Sundays, 9 a.m.–2 p.m.), a market with a global vibe so pronounced that the posters and website that advertise it are rendered in five languages. The scope of its offerings has started to draw shoppers from far-off neighborhoods who are eager to try something new or are hunting down a hard-to-find specialty item. Compared with some of the other Portland farmers markets, it's on the small side, but it has a distinctive community-based feel that can't be missed.

Another block up, past a Mexican restaurant, is the formerly dodgy-looking bar that has been reborn as the ❸ Eagle Eye Tavern, a fun, slightly hipsterized neighborhood hangout with pool tables, pinball, and a lively crowd on weekend nights. From here you can see a number of the massive new developments that have been going up near this corner recently, most of which are apartments and condos with retail spaces on the ground floor. All the development is bound to change the vibe of the area rather quickly—hopefully in a positive direction. Case in point: At the intersection of Southeast 92nd Avenue and Southeast Foster Road, the block that used to be home to a notoriously sketchy but weirdly iconic nightclub called the New Copper Penny was finally, after decades of bargaining, sold to developers in 2016, allowing that parcel of land to be included in the city's redevelopment plans. It is now home to one of the new mixed-use apartment buildings springing up all over this part of Lents.

Cross back over to the other side of Southeast Foster Road, and take the walkway left up to the Lents/Southeast Foster MAX Station, where you can catch the Green Line back into town. From here, you can also hop onto the I-205 multiuse path, either on foot or bicycle, and follow it south a few blocks until it meets the paved Springwater Corridor Trail. You can take the trail in either direction: Turn right and you'll end up at the Willamette River near the suburb of Milwaukie (see Walk 32, page 158, for more about that area). Turn left and the trail meanders east alongside creeks, parks, and strip malls in almost equal measure, to the little town of Boring, where it ends.

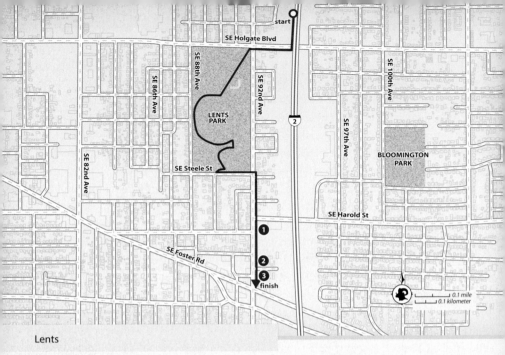

Lents

Points of Interest

1 Belmont Goats belmontgoats.org

2 Lents International Farmers Market lentsfarmersmarket.org, SE 92nd Ave. and Foster Rd.

3 Eagle Eye Tavern 5836 SE 92nd Ave., 503-774-2141

28 Reed College and Woodstock
Communism, Atheism, Free Love

Above: Stroll through the campus of Reed College, where Steve Jobs attended.

BOUNDARIES: SE Woodstock Blvd., SE 28th Ave., SE 47th Ave., SE Steele St.
DISTANCE: 2.5 miles (not including optional Crystal Springs Rhododendron Garden detour)
DIFFICULTY: Easy
PARKING: On street, small lot on campus
PUBLIC TRANSIT: TriMet Bus 75 (SE Cesar Chavez Blvd. and Harold or Knight St.) or Bus 19
  (SE Woodstock Blvd. and 46th Ave.)

Reed College occupies a beautiful campus surrounded by an equally attractive residential neighborhood. Founded in 1908 and named for Oregon pioneers Simeon and Amanda Reed, the school is uniquely and legendarily progressive. (Its unofficial motto is "Communism, Atheism, Free Love.") Apple founder Steve Jobs famously dropped out—he often credited a calligraphy class he took at Reed with helping him figure out computer fonts and backgrounds. Other notable Reedies include journalist Barbara Ehrenreich, poet Gary Snyder, and (briefly) musician

Ry Cooder. The students here work their tails off (Reed produces disproportionately high numbers of Rhodes Scholars and PhDs and is notorious for academic rigor), but anyone can enjoy strolling the grounds without so much as setting foot in a library. Add in a side trip through Crystal Springs Rhododendron Garden before you head up the hill into the heart of the charming Woodstock neighborhood.

Walk Description

Start at the bus stop at Southeast 39th Avenue and Southeast Harold Street. Head south on 39th Avenue, then turn right onto Southeast Reedway Avenue. Walk down the hill on Reedway to Southeast 38th Avenue, and find the little dirt trail that leads down into the woods. This path winds through Reed Canyon, alongside Crystal Springs Creek and around Reed Lake. The canyon is a 28-acre watershed that essentially bisects the ❶ **Reed College** campus. It's home to a range of interesting plants and wild animals (and no, I don't mean the students—more like garter snakes and birds). At the fork, bear right and follow the trail as it meanders around the north side of Reed Lake. Eventually you'll come to a gray concrete-and-steel bridge; don't cross it, but pass underneath it and continue along the trail.

The trail ends when it meets a gravel road. Turn left here and walk through a small parking lot, then up the stairs. You'll be facing Cerf Auditorium, built in 1936 and named for a Reed literature professor. Keeping the auditorium to your left, walk up the hill along the cement path. Stay on the path as it sweeps left, across the top of the auditorium, then sneaks behind a large gray building. Keep your eye on the windows to your right as you walk by, and you'll catch a glimpse of a mural of comic-book characters, including *Transmetropolitan*'s Spider Jerusalem: this is the entrance to the totally awesome Reed comics library, called the MLLL (mlll.org—the website has a pretty useful comic-book-recommendation engine).

Follow the cement path around the corner of the building, uphill, and to the right. You'll emerge onto the lawn behind the Student Union; to your left is Eliot Hall. Walk straight ahead onto the Great Lawn, a vast, open, tree-dotted area that's ideal for a picnic, reading, napping, maybe some croquet, or just appreciating the lovely campus, whose plan was loosely modeled on St. John's College at Oxford.

Eliot Hall—more or less the architectural centerpiece of the campus—was built in 1912, in the same Tudor Gothic style that defines the other impressive building you see from the lawn, Old Dorm Block. Look for the Reed College seal over the southwest corner of Eliot Hall; it incorporates roses as well as fleurs-de-lis from Washington University in St. Louis, where Thomas Lamb

Eliot went to school. There are 13 stars borrowed from the family crest of John Adams, a relative of Amanda Reed. The griffin on the seal is Reed's unofficial mascot—it has a lion's body with an eagle's head and is associated with protection and wisdom. Eliot himself was that rare creature, a powerful clergyman in the Pacific Northwest. He came to Portland in 1867 to serve as minister at the large new Unitarian Church. He worked for a number of progressive causes, including education, child welfare, and women's suffrage, and he served on the Reed College board of trustees for 20 years. Adding to his brainy bona fides, he was the uncle of literary giant T. S. Eliot.

Eliot Hall is also where the Reed experience culminates, at least academically: seniors have to write a thesis in order to graduate, and it's a rigorous undertaking. So each year at the end of the semester, all the seniors who managed to complete it make two extra copies of their thesis (having turned in the real one already) and embark on the Thesis Parade, in which a ragtag marching band leads the seniors into Eliot Hall and up to the registrar's office, where one by one they each plunk down their thesis, symbolically and with much fanfare handing it in. (The second extra copy is then ceremoniously burned in a bonfire right in front of the library.) Then everyone gets drunk and high in the rain.

From the Great Lawn, in front of Eliot Hall and Old Dorm Block, wander downhill (west) between Anna Mann (the pretty gray dorm to your right) and McNaughton (a newer, less pretty dorm) toward the campus's West Parking Lot. (This slope is usually the location of the naked waterslide during Reed's annual Renn Fayre, FYI.) Carefully cross the street (Southeast 28th Avenue) to the entrance of ❷ Crystal Springs Rhododendron Garden.

If time allows, Crystal Springs makes for a very pleasant detour. Once upon a time, the land now occupied by the garden was Crystal Springs Farm, owned by William Ladd, of Ladd's Addition and Laurelhurst Park fame (see Backstory: William S. Ladd, page 69). Before it became a botanical garden, it was used as an outdoor theater (Reedies apparently used to call it Shakespeare Island). The land found its true calling in the 1950s, as a botanical test garden. Over the years it has gradually been developed, shaped, and landscaped (partly using rocks from Mount Hood) and now contains some 2,500 azaleas, rhododendrons, and other plants. Mostly it's just a really pretty place to wander around, look at some fountains, see masses of surrealistically colorful flowers in bloom, and so forth.

Leaving the garden, take a right on Southeast 28th Avenue and then a left onto Southeast Woodstock Boulevard. Follow Woodstock up the hill, alongside a residential area of upscale homes and quiet, tree-lined side streets. Cross Southeast 39th Avenue at the stoplight at the hill's summit, and continue along Woodstock Boulevard. On your right as you cross 39th Avenue, you'll see a once dilapidated and now semi-fixed-up yellowy-beige house on the corner—this storied house long served as a Reed party house called the Dustbin, where many good times have been forgotten.

At Southeast 43rd Avenue, look left to peek at the ❸ **Woodstock Community Center.** It's housed in a restored firehouse from 1928 and holds classes for kids and adults alike, in everything from Tae Kwon Do to finger painting.

Lots of eating and drinking establishments line this stretch of Woodstock, but one of the friendlier and livelier options is the ❹ **Delta Cafe,** just past Southeast 46th Avenue, where you can get Southern home cooking and a 40-ounce bottle of Pabst Blue Ribbon served in a bucket of ice like Champagne.

Before or after visiting the Delta, pop in at the ❺ **Lutz Tavern,** a beloved Reed student hangout next door. Several changes in ownership have left it looking like a bar in search of an identity, but it has a long history and an easygoing vibe.

Retrace your steps back down the hill to Southeast 39th Avenue, turn right, and reach the starting point, or catch a bus at Woodstock Boulevard and 46th Avenue toward downtown.

The back side of Eliot Hall at Reed College

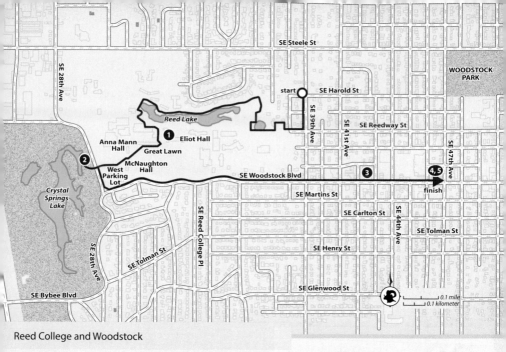

Reed College and Woodstock

Points of Interest

1 Reed College reed.edu, 3203 SE Woodstock Blvd., 503-771-1112

2 Crystal Springs Rhododendron Garden rhodies.org, SE 28th Ave. and Woodstock Blvd., 503-771-8386

3 Woodstock Community Center 5905 SE 43rd Ave., 503-823-3633

4 Delta Cafe deltacafepdx.com, 4607 SE Woodstock Blvd., 503-771-3101

5 Lutz Tavern lutztavern.com, 4639 SE Woodstock Blvd., 503-774-0353

29 Sellwood
Antique Jungle

Above: The Johnson Jewelers clock and the 1926 Moreland Theater are neighborhood landmarks.

BOUNDARIES: SE Milwaukie Ave., SE Tacoma St., Willamette River
DISTANCE: 4 miles
DIFFICULTY: Easy–moderate
PARKING: Small free lot at start/finish; nearby street parking also available
PUBLIC TRANSIT: TriMet Bus 19 (numerous stops along SE Milwaukie Ave.)

Annexed by Portland in 1893, Sellwood for many years was its own incorporated town, and it still has the independent, off-the-main-drag feel of "elsewhere." The neighborhood is known primarily for Antique Row, the nickname for Southeast 13th Avenue, although these days many of the antiques stores along the street have been replaced by restaurants and coffee shops. Sellwood's other claim to fame is Oaks Amusement Park, a charmingly low-key family-fun spot with year-round roller skating, and the abutting Oaks Bottom Wildlife Refuge, a great place for bird-watching. The trail through the refuge is part of the Springwater Corridor trail network, which in turn is part of the metro area's 40-Mile Loop trail system. (The Springwater Trail currently runs 21 miles from industrial Southeast Portland to the town of Boring; plans call for eventually connecting it to the Pacific Crest Trail.) The new-in-2016 Sellwood Bridge is Portland's southernmost; it replaced the original from 1925, partly to improve earthquake-readiness.

Walk Description

Start at the small parking lot for ❶ **Oaks Bottom Wildlife Refuge,** where Southeast Milwaukie Avenue meets Mitchell Street, just north of Sellwood proper. The refuge includes about 160 acres of woodlands and wetlands and serves as home or landing strip to more than a hundred bird species. A paved footpath descends into the woodlands between Sellwood and the river. After about 500 meters, the pavement swoops right, toward the river and the Springwater Trail—instead, you'll take the Bluff Trail, a narrower dirt path that continues straight.

About 800 meters farther along, look uphill to your left to see the backside of ❷ **Wilhelm's Portland Memorial Funeral Home,** which has been cheerily brightened up with paintings of birds on the lake (but remains, somehow, just a little creepy). The opposite side of the trail here is a dense marshland that feels quite far from the bustling neighborhood just over the ridge.

After circling the marsh, the Bluff Trail runs smack into the Springwater Trail at ❸ **Oaks Amusement Park.** Here you'll find a roller-skating rink, carnival rides, go-karts, bumper cars, and a well-worn collection of midway entertainments. If you stop in, don't miss the hand-carved wooden carousel from 1912.

Continue south along the Springwater Trail until you reach the tiny ❹ **Oaks Pioneer Church,** at Southeast Spokane Street. Born in 1851 as the St. Johns Episcopal Church in Milwaukie (south of Sellwood), the little white building moved twice before settling here. After 10 years it was scooted closer to Southeast Main Street in Milwaukie. Then, in 1883, the church got a remodel, adding its current stained glass windows and steeple. In the 1950s it moved again, to Southeast Jefferson Street in Milwaukie, where it served as a Sunday-school annex to a larger church building and suffered the indignity of having linoleum floors installed. But its big adventure came in the 1960s, when it was spared from demolition and instead shipped by barge up the Willamette River to its current home, where (linoleum-free) it's a popular spot for weddings and funerals.

Walk up the hill along Southeast Spokane Street until you reach Southeast 13th Avenue. If you're in need of sustenance, try ❺ **Gino's,** on the corner. It's a beautiful old family-style Italian restaurant with a lovely bar. Otherwise, turn left and continue north on 13th Avenue into the heart of Sellwood.

Southeast 13th Avenue is Sellwood's Antique Row, lined with antiques shops (though these days they battle for space with new restaurants and coffee shops). There's a pretty good range of inventory, from high-end and rare items to cardboard boxes full of broken Legos and one-legged baby dolls. A good place to start is ❻ **The Sellwood Antique Collective,** a block past Gino's, where several vendors are gathered under one roof.

A few blocks farther, at Southeast Bidwell Street, is the ❼ **Sellwood-Moreland branch of the Multnomah County Library.** Started in 1905 as the Sellwood Reading Room with 100 books, in a small building on Nehalem Street, the library moved into this successful experiment in mixed-use architecture in 2002. The building also contains commercial space and 16 condominiums.

Continue along Southeast 13th Avenue until it rounds a bend and, at Southeast 14th Avenue, becomes Southeast Bybee Boulevard. Here you can also peek into the pretty grounds of the somewhat-less-creepy Memorial Funeral Home. Follow Southeast Bybee Boulevard until it meets Southeast Milwaukie Avenue (at which point those so inclined may want to duck half a block right for another antiques powerhouse, ❽ **Stars Antiques Mall**). Turn left on Milwaukie Avenue to walk through the tiny heart of Sellwood.

One of Portland's handful of historic single-screen movie houses, the 1926 ❾ **Moreland Theater,** is on the right. Look for the Johnson Jewelers clock, a familiar landmark, out front.

Continuing along Southeast Milwaukie Avenue, you'll find plenty of chances for refreshment, but wait until you reach the yin–yang duo that is ❿ **Papa Haydn** and the ⓫ **Yukon Tavern.** The former is a delightfully upscale restaurant known for its desserts, with a lovely outdoor garden in the warmer months; the Yukon, on the other hand, is an excellent dive with faded red-velvet walls, cheap drinks, and ancient regulars glued to their disintegrating barstools. You really can't lose either way.

From here, make your way along Southeast Milwaukie Avenue back to the walk's starting point at the Oaks Bottom parking lot.

Connecting the Walks

The Springwater Corridor Trail continues north into Portland proper, near the Oregon Museum of Science and Industry (OMSI), where you can link with **Walk 12: Industrial Southeast** (page 59).

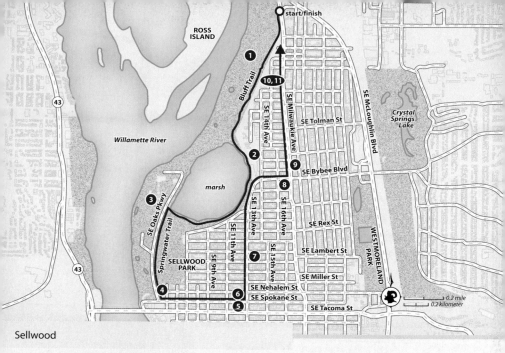

Sellwood

Points of Interest

1 Oaks Bottom Wildlife Refuge tinyurl.com/oaksbottom, SE Milwaukie Ave. and Mitchell St.

2 Wilhelm's Portland Memorial Funeral Home 6705 SE 14th Ave.

3 Oaks Amusement Park oakspark.com, 7805 SE Oaks Park Way, 503-233-5777

4 Oaks Pioneer Church oakspioneerchurch.org, 455 SE Spokane St.

5 Gino's ginossellwood.com, 8051 SE 13th Ave., 503-233-4613

6 Sellwood Antique Collective sellwoodcollective.blogspot.com, 8027 SE 13th Ave., 503-736-1399

7 Sellwood-Moreland Library multcolib.org, 7860 SE 13th Ave., 503-988-5398

8 Stars Antiques Mall starsantique.com, 7030 SE Milwaukie Ave., 503-239-0346

9 Moreland Theater morelandtheater.com, 6712 SE Milwaukie Ave., 503-236-5257

10 Papa Haydn papahaydn.com, 5829 SE Milwaukie Ave., 503-232-9440

11 Yukon Tavern yukontavern.com, 5819 SE Milwaukie Ave., 503-235-6352

30 Multnomah Village
Small but Filling

Above: Multnomah Antique Gallery

BOUNDARIES: SW Vermont St., SW 45th Ave., SW Multnomah Blvd., SW 30th Ave.
DISTANCE: 1.75 miles
DIFFICULTY: Easy
PARKING: Free street parking, lots at Gabriel Park
PUBLIC TRANSIT: TriMet Buses 1 and 45 (SW Vermont St. and 37th Ave.) or Bus 44
   (SW Capitol Hwy. and 33rd Ave.)

Built around an Oregon Electric Railway depot and annexed by Portland in 1950, Multnomah Village is a cute, pocket-size neighborhood just out of the way enough to be neglected by many Portlanders. It feels like a trek from the city center, but in fact it's only about 5 miles from downtown and easily accessible by bus. The neighborhood's core is a very compact area with a surprising variety of shops, bars, and cafés. And the surrounding areas are lovely—thick with trees and rich in green spaces, including nearby Gabriel Park, where our walk begins. Though Multnomah

Village is an easy drive from Portland proper, I recommend using public transportation if you can, particularly if you plan to take advantage of the neighborhood's disproportionately high number of excellent dive bars. This is a point-to-point walk with bus stops at either end, so playing it safe should be easy.

Walk Description

Start the walk at the northeast corner of Gabriel Park—there's a bus stop here and another a few blocks east. The path forks a few feet from the entrance; take the right-hand branch and follow its meandering path across to the west side of the park. Gabriel Park is a 90-acre playground with something for just about everyone. Paved and dirt trails wind all across the park, and you'll also find the usual picnic areas, ball fields, tennis courts, basketball courts, and dog parks. There's a state-of-the-art play area for the little kids, and a skate park, built in 2008, for the slightly bigger kids. Along with a community garden, there's a demonstration orchard. The park is named after a farmer who once owned this land (back in the 1890s), a Swiss immigrant named Ulrich Gabriel.

At the baseball field, take the left fork to pass the skate park. Follow the path between two tennis courts and continue straight as it heads into a more thickly forested area. This section of path winds through the woods for a while; you'll come out near a small baseball diamond. Pass this and continue to a small parking lot, at the southeast corner of the park.

Exit the park by taking a left onto Southwest Canby Street. Turn right on Southwest 40th Avenue, walk one block, then turn left onto Southwest Troy Street, which you'll follow into the tiny Multnomah Village town center.

When you reach Southwest 35th Avenue, turn right. Cross over Southwest Capitol Highway and continue straight along Southwest 35th. Here on your left are a few cute shops and cafés, and on your right, ❶ **The Ship Tavern.** The Ship is an old Multnomah Village standby—a vaguely nautically themed dive with pool tables and sports on TV. The floor is usually covered in peanut shells, which gives the place a nice crunch. There's nothing even remotely fancy about The Ship, and it's not necessarily a place you want to go for food (most people just stick with the peanuts), but it's a great neighborhood bar all the same.

Leaving The Ship, continue down Southwest 35th Avenue to Southwest Multnomah Boulevard and turn right. At the corner is ❷ **John's Market,** known far and wide for its vast selection of rare, imported, seasonal, and just top-notch bottled beer and wine (it claims the largest selection in Portland), as well as kegs of hard-to-find imported beer. There's also a good deli here.

Where Multnomah meets Southwest Capitol Highway in an acute angle, turn right on Capitol to walk along the main commercial center of the village. For its size, Multnomah Village has a remarkably large number of good places in which to eat and drink—mostly the latter. On your right you'll see the Multnomah Commercial and Savings Bank building, formerly home to longstanding neighborhood pub O'Connor's, whose owner retired in 2018. Before it moved to Multnomah Village, O'Connor's was located in downtown Portland; it was founded in 1934, by Ed O'Connor of Butte, Montana. The original spot's dubious claim to fame is that, according to its website, it was one of the very last men-only bars in Portland. Rumor has it that a new restaurant and whiskey bar will be opening soon in the space.

A couple of doors down is ❸ Annie Bloom's Books, established in 1978 and one of the coziest, most inviting independent bookshops in Portland. There's a store cat, of course, and the shop regularly hosts author readings.

The historic Fat City Cafe

Also on this strip is the well-loved ❹ Fat City Cafe, a neighborhood diner serving greasy-spoon breakfasts in a kitsch-plastered space. The food might not be all that memorable, but the diner has a permanent place in local history, thanks to what has come to be known as the Fat City Firing. In 1987, then-Mayor Bud Clark was sitting here having breakfast with his police chief when whatever conversation they were having ended in Clark's famous remark, "Read my lips: you're fired." Look for a sign over one of the booths commemorating the dismissal.

Across the street is another great local dive, ❺ Renner's Grill, boasting one of the coolest neon signs in the area. It has everything you need in a dive bar: cheap, strong drinks; fried food; friendly locals; and not much else. A kitchen fire in 2018 caused enough damage that the place had to close temporarily for repairs and cleaning, but most of the interior, furnishings, and decor were

Annie Bloom's Books

preserved. As this book went to press, the owners were working to get the place reopened, but the age of the building meant there were a lot of obstacles, so cross your fingers.

Continue along Southwest Capitol Highway and cross over Southwest 35th Avenue. If you're in the mood to browse, pop into the Multnomah Antique Gallery, in a cute little building on the right. Walk several blocks (noting a stop for Bus 44 as you pass Southwest 33rd Avenue—you'll want to come back to this stop when you've finished the walk). When you reach Southwest 32nd Avenue, you'll see on your left the ❻ **Lucky Labrador Public House,** which occupies a 1925 Masonic Temple. (There are also Lucky Lab locations in Northwest Portland and on Southeast Hawthorne Boulevard.) Feel free to cross the street and stop in for a pint, or continue straight along Capitol Highway for one more block.

Duck right just briefly onto Southwest Canby Street to find ❼ **Otto & Anita's Schnitzel Haus,** an adorable European-style restaurant with a menu of various homemade schnitzels and other Bavarian specialties; it might be the only place around where you can satisfy your craving for dill-pickle soup.

Return to the city center by hopping TriMet Bus 44 back to town; there's a stop at Southwest Capitol Highway and 33rd Avenue, diagonally across the street from the Lucky Lab. (If you drove a car to the starting point and parked at Gabriel Park, simply retrace your steps and cut through the park to return to the parking lot.)

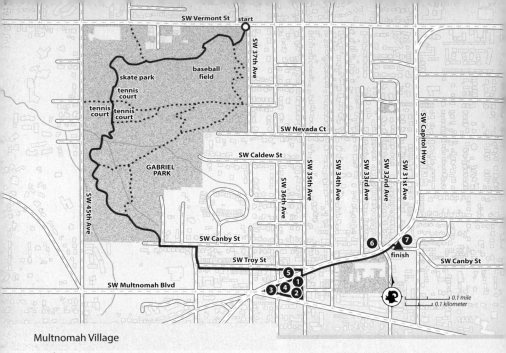

Multnomah Village

Points of Interest

1. **The Ship Tavern** mvship.com, 7827 SW 35th Ave., 503-244-7345

2. **John's Market** johnsmarketplace.com, 3535 SW Multnomah Blvd., 503-244-2617

3. **Annie Bloom's Books** annieblooms.com, 7834 SW Capitol Hwy., 503-246-0053

4. **Fat City Cafe** 7820 SW Capitol Hwy., 503-245-5457

5. **Renner's Grill** rennersgrill.com, 7819 SW Capitol Hwy., 503-246-9097

6. **Lucky Labrador Public House** luckylab.com, 7675 SW Capitol Hwy., 503-244-2537

7. **Otto & Anita's Schnitzel Haus** ottoandanitas.com, 3025 SW Canby St., 503-452-1411

31 Fernhill Park to Woodlawn
Trees and Shrubs, Parks and Pubs

Above: Fernhill Park

BOUNDARIES: NE 42nd Ave., NE Sixth Ave., NE Dekum St., NE Killingsworth St.
DISTANCE: 3 miles
DIFFICULTY: Easy
PARKING: Free street parking
PUBLIC TRANSIT: TriMet Buses 6, 8, 17, 75

With its aggressively artsy, hipster-burrito and artisan ice-cream scene, this low-key part of town just a few blocks north of busy Northeast Alberta Street is beginning to change, but for now it remains a fairly diverse, mostly working-class residential neighborhood bookmarked by two large, lovely parks, with another one right in the middle. It wasn't always the nicest place to visit. The Woodlawn neighborhood especially was plagued by drugs, gangs, and prostitution starting in the 1970s and peaking around the mid-'90s. As recently as 2009, *The Oregonian* described the area as "ragged" and "run-down," but it did so in the context of describing a turnaround—a process that continues to this day. You could look at Woodlawn as an example of a much quieter, gentler, more organic version of the gentrification that's happening or has happened in so many Northeast Portland neighborhoods. Houses here have always been on the smaller side, meaning they're at least reasonably close to being within reach for average Portland homebuyers, and the businesses that cluster around the Dekum Triangle tend to be locally owned and neighborhood-focused.

Along beautiful Ainsworth Street, the tree-lined avenue that runs east to west between Fernhill Park and Alberta Park, houses start to get a little fancier, but the thick margin of green that goes right down the middle of the street keeps things quiet and scenic. In fact, it almost makes the street feel like yet another park.

Other than the Kennedy School, which we're shoehorning into this route just because it's so close by, nothing here is a big draw for tourists; there are

Beautiful tree-lined Ainsworth Street connects Fernhill and Alberta Parks.

closer-in locations of the famous Breakside Brewery, for example. For the most part, people come to Woodlawn because they want to be here. Wander over yourself and find out why.

Walk Description

Start the walk at the southeast corner of ❶ Fernhill Park, a vast expanse edged by impressive old trees, with a huge off-leash dog run, a new kid-friendly water park, a running track, tennis courts, and a grassy gulley that, rumor has it, was once a dumping ground for stolen cars, back in the bad old days. There are worse ways to spend a hot day than to get yourself "accidentally" splashed in the water park and then find a shady spot beneath a huge old tree and sit for a while.

After exploring the park's various corners, make your way among the strollers and dog walkers to its west side, at the corner of Northeast 37th Avenue and Northeast Ainsworth Street. Continue walking west along Ainsworth, a wide, pretty, tree-lined avenue that's ideal for a quiet stroll. At Northeast 33rd Avenue, go left (south) for a block and a half to reach the somewhat conspicuous

② McMenamins Kennedy School. The Kennedy School is an old elementary-school building from 1915 that has been converted, in classic McMenamins style, to a hotel-bar-cinema-entertainment complex—because who hasn't dreamed of spending a night in your grade-school classroom? Detention is a whiskey bar, as it should be, and there are numerous other food and drink venues, as well as the movie theater, courtyard seating, and a soaking pool, all decorated with the Portland chain's signature neo-hippie, slightly goofy but charming artwork.

Having refreshed yourself (or just wandered the halls aimlessly, trying to remember your locker combination *again*), retrace your steps back to Northeast Ainsworth Street and turn left (west). In a few blocks you'll come to **③ Alberta Park,** with its tall shade trees and a nice walking and jogging path that goes all the way around, plus tennis courts and covered picnic areas. Hang out here as long as you like.

Leaving the park from its northeast corner, walk north along Northeast 22nd Avenue about five blocks until you reach Northeast Dekum Street. Take a left on Dekum, and in the next block you'll see the **④ Tough Luck** on your right. Run by the people responsible for the popular Old Gold in North Portland and the Paydirt whiskey bar in Southeast, this cool neo-industrial space inhabits a 1960s-era building renovated to look a bit like a chic garage. There's a massive wall of booze behind the bar, a decent food menu with some unexpected choices alongside the classic burgers and fries (poached albacore with yuzu mayo; Malaysian shrimp skewers), and a great wraparound patio for outdoor seating.

Alberta Park

Continue walking west along Dekum Street. Just past Northeast 13th Avenue, veer slightly right onto Northeast Claremont Avenue, and you'll end up smack in the middle of Woodlawn City Park. There's a splash pad, a playground, tennis courts, baseball and soccer fields, walking and jogging paths, a community garden, and an amphitheater for live music, movie screenings, and other events.

The park is the centerpiece of the historic Woodlawn Conservation District, a designation the city bestows to help preserve the character of historically significant neighborhoods. This area was originally settled in the 1860s as a farming town, and only much later was it absorbed into greater Portland. During the 1950s, many of the people who were displaced from the flooded Vanport neighborhood ended up moving here. (See Walk 26: Columbia River Walk, page 130, for more of that story.)

Having thoroughly explored the park, head back out onto Northeast Dekum Street. Where it meets Northeast Durham Avenue, you'll find a small cluster of businesses at the tip of what locals call the Dekum Triangle (or sometimes the Woodlawn Triangle, although this doesn't quite seem to have caught on). There are several worthwhile stops here, but you'd be silly to pass up the chance for a pint at ❺ **Breakside Brewery.** The craft brewer's Wanderlust is a West Coast–style IPA and highly recommended, and there are usually a bunch of seasonal beers on tap that are well worth trying. The food is good too.

In the same block is Firehouse Restaurant, which was one of the first businesses to open in this neighborhood. At the time, it was a run-down fire station when Mathew Busetto, a chef who worked at ClarkLewis restaurant, decided the area needed a pizza joint. (Busetto has since retired and sold the place, but its long-established menu and neighborhood vibe are still going strong.) A handful of other businesses started up around the same time, including Good Neighbor Pizza, a local favorite. Across the street is The Woodlawn, a large gray apartment building with some cool design features, including vertical strips of live plants growing up the walls, and the busy Grand Army Tavern on the ground level.

If you'd like to conclude your walk with a final pint but also want to feel like you're helping to improve the world, consider stopping in at the ❻ **Oregon Public House.** This comfy, family-friendly pub is run as a nonprofit, which allows it to donate its proceeds to a wide variety of charities. It chooses six nonprofits to partner with every few months, then switches it up, so your cheeseburger, sweet potato tots, and pint of fresh-hopped cider may end up supporting anything from the Northeast Portland Tool Library to a mental-health advocacy program to study-abroad scholarships for low-income students.

Fernhill Park to Woodlawn

Points of Interest

1. Fernhill Park portlandoregon.gov/parks, NE 37th Ave. and Ainsworth St., 503-823-2525
2. McMenamins Kennedy School mcmenamins.com/kennedy-school, 5736 NE 33rd Ave., 503-249-3983
3. Alberta Park portlandoregon.gov/parks, 1905 NE Killingsworth St., 503-823-7529
4. Tough Luck toughluckbar.com, 1771 NE Dekum St., 971-754-4188
5. Breakside Brewery breakside.com, 820 NE Dekum St., 503-719-6475
6. Oregon Public House oregonpublichouse.com, 700 NE Dekum St., 503-828-0884

32 Milwaukie
Bing It On!

Above: Explore Elk Rock Island in the Willamette Narrows.

BOUNDARIES: SE Sparrow St., Willamette River, OR 224, and SE 24th Ave.
DISTANCE: 3 miles
DIFFICULTY: Easy
PARKING: Free and metered street parking
PUBLIC TRANSIT: TriMet Buses 29 and 33 and MAX Orange Line

There are a lot of noteworthy things about this Portland suburb, but probably the most important one is that it's the birthplace of the Bing cherry, surely one of the best fruits ever cultivated.
The Bing cherry took its name from Ah Bing, a Manchurian Chinese foreman who oversaw the
orchards where this type of cherry was developed in the late 1800s. Milwaukie itself, as you might
guess, was named after the city in Wisconsin (which used to be spelled that way, too, sometimes,
before the current spelling won out). To a different crowd, it's also known as the headquarters of
Dark Horse Comics (publishers of *Hellboy, Sin City, Buffy the Vampire Slayer,* and a ton of other titles

you'd recognize, plus the last graphic novel Anthony Bourdain wrote before he died), which now occupies a good-size chunk of Main Street. The downtown core of this neighborhood is small, compact, and sort of charmingly old-fashioned (or, more precisely, it's not especially fashionable and not too worried about it). A brand-new, manicured waterfront park adds opportunities for picnicking and river access. And then there's Elk Rock Island, an odd little nub of land that sticks out into the Willamette River and can be reached on foot when the water level is low.

Once upon a time, Milwaukie was connected to Portland (and even as far as Troutdale and Estacada) by the Interurban Trolley Line. The trolley ran for 65 years, until the Portland Transit Company abandoned it in 1958. But now, Milwaukie and Portland are linked once again, thanks to TriMet's Orange Line, so it's easier than ever to explore.

Walk Description

Start the walk by taking the MAX Orange Line to the Milwaukie Main Street station. Nestled up against the rail line is a food-cart pod (called Milwaukie Station), with about a dozen food carts and one that serves beer and cider, plus restrooms and covered picnic areas. Not a bad place to wait for the train!

From the station, walk north up Southeast Main Street for two blocks, then turn left on Southeast Washington Street to reach a crosswalk at the intersection with busy Southeast McLoughlin Boulevard (aka OR 99E, whose proper name is the much more exciting McLoughlin Super Highway). Cross over and walk toward the edge of the water, where you'll find a paved bicycle path that traces its way south (left) along the river. This path runs into Southeast 19th Avenue; you continue walking straight (south) along Southeast 19th Avenue until it crosses Southeast Sparrow Street at the edge of the Spring Park. Here you turn right (west) onto any of several informal footpaths that will lead you across a low, rocky stretch of land and onto ❶ Elk Rock Island. This can be tricky if winter and spring rains have raised the water level too high, so be sure to use common sense as you pick your way across, and don't step where you can't see your footing.

Elk Rock Island is typical of the geological features that characterize the Willamette Narrows, this section of the river. It's rocky and thin-soiled, with just enough of a top layer to support a patch of gnarled oak trees and prairie grass. The island and others like it are generally thought to have been formed during the Missoula Floods, some 15,000 years ago, give or take. The rocky cliffs you cross to reach the island are made of basalt that was later covered in lava, creating a surface hard enough to withstand the river's current for eons while other lava deposits around it were eaten away. This pattern created lots of small "tidepools" in the rock at the edges of the islands—fun to explore, especially for curious kids. A network of trails lets you walk all around the tiny island (keeping an eye out for poison oak), but to get an even better view, consider borrowing a kayak and checking it out from the water. Supposedly, a peregrine falcon keeps a nest on the opposite shore, but so far your author hasn't been lucky enough to spot it.

Once you've explored the little island to your heart's content, retrace your steps, heading back north to ❷ **Milwaukie Riverfront Park** and recrossing Southeast McLoughlin Boulevard on Southeast Washington Street. From here, turn left (north) to go up Southeast Main Street.

Just past Southeast Jefferson Street, you'll pass ❸ **Things From Another World,** a fun comic book and novelties shop, on the left, and then the ❹ **Dark Horse Comics** offices on the right. In two more blocks, look for the ❺ **Milwaukie City Hall,** built in the mid-1930s, on the right. On the left is the site of the local weekly farmers market, held on Sunday mornings.

Continue north on Southeast Main Street until you see two iconic buildings on the right: Pietro's Pizza, a vividly red-and-white-striped candy box of a place packed with games and fabulous prizes, and ❻ **Kellogg Bowl,** an old-school bowling alley that might be a little run-down but feeds the nostalgia beast. (If you want to feed anything else, though, you'll need to order pizza from next door.)

As you leave Kellogg Bowl, head east from the large parking lot over to Southeast 23rd Avenue. Turn right (south). Southeast 23rd Ave becomes Southeast Harrison Street, which starts to curve around to the west; but first, take a quick detour to see the ❼ **Ledding Library** complex, off to your right. The library is named for Florence Ledding (1870–1961), one of the first women to work as an attorney in Oregon. Ledding established the collection on her property and handed it over to the city. The library's Pond House contains a used-book store that benefits library operations. Both library buildings sit beside a manicured pond fed by Spring Creek and are pleasant to walk around. At the time of this writing, the library was about to begin a renovation, so its normal hours and facilities might not apply; check ahead.

Just south of the library entrance, Southeast Harrison Street meets Southeast 21st Avenue. Turn left onto Southeast 21st Avenue, continuing south. You'll now pass behind the Milwaukie City Hall we visited earlier, as well as Dark Horse Comics. In a few blocks you'll reach ❽ **Duffy's Irish Pub** on the left. It's nothing fancy and is more sports-oriented than particularly Irish-seeming, but it's a friendly place with a good list of beers on tap and cheap drink specials, if you're so inclined.

From Duffy's Irish Pub it's just another two blocks south on Southeast 21st Avenue to reach the MAX light-rail station where our walk began.

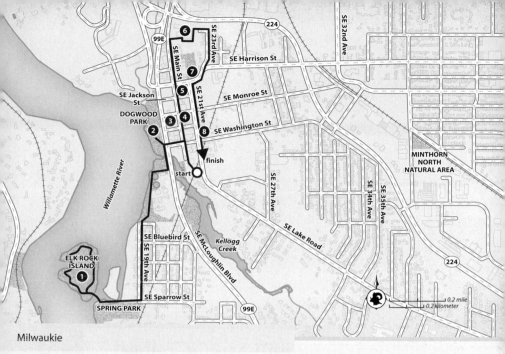

Milwaukie

Points of Interest

1. Elk Rock Island SE 19th Ave. and SE Sparrow St.
2. Milwaukie Riverfront Park 11211 SE McLoughlin Blvd.
3. Things From Another World tfaw.com, 10977 SE Main St., 503-652-2752
4. Dark Horse Comics darkhorse.com, 10956 SE Main St., 503-654-4184
5. Milwaukie City Hall milwaukieoregon.gov, 10722 SE Main St., 503-786-7555
6. Kellogg Bowl kelloggbowl.com, 10306 SE Main St., 503-659-1757
7. Ledding Library milwaukieoregon.gov/library, 10660 SE 21st Ave., 503-786-7580
8. Duffy's Irish Pub duffyspdx.com, 11050 SE 21st Ave., 503-344-6553

33 Mount Scott and Mount Talbert
Shifting Perspectives

Above: A trail in Mount Scott Nature Park

BOUNDARIES: I-205, SE Summers Lane, SE 122nd Ave., SE Idleman Road
DISTANCE: 5 miles
DIFFICULTY: Moderate
PARKING: Free parking in lots and on street
PUBLIC TRANSIT: TriMet Bus 155

Maybe it's ironic, maybe it's lucky, or maybe it's the result of good planning, but some of the most pristine woods in the Portland area spring up out of some of the busiest, fastest-growing, and most heavily trafficked suburban commercial zones. We're talking shopping malls, banks, Jamba Juice, Starbucks, and RiteAid, all clustered around two forested hillsides laced with creeks and trails. This figure-eight loop explores these protected natural areas, Mount Talbert and Mount Scott, which stick out of the busy commercial strip and offer great views as well as plenty of breathing room for urban hikers. The Metro regional government has been planning and building trails and corridors to help connect these and several nearby nature parks into one cohesive trail system for nonmotorized traffic. The end goal is a loop trail that will connect the well-established Springwater Corridor Trail with existing trail networks on Mount Scott, Mount Talbert, Powell Butte, and Scouters Mountain Nature Park, extending all the way to the Clackamas River area in the south. For now, some of these links are only conceptual; we'll use our imagination.

Keep in mind that although this walk passes near all the conveniences of a modern suburban shopping zone, it doesn't really go through it, so plan to bring whatever supplies you'll need, including snacks, water, and rain gear, or pick them up before you set out from the starting point.

Walk Description

Start in the middle of the figure eight, at the northeast corner of ❶ **Mount Talbert Nature Park.** There's a TriMet bus stop on Southeast 117th Avenue along Sunnyside Road, about a block from the trailhead parking lot. Right away the trail crosses a bridge over Mount Scott Creek. After heading uphill for a stretch, you'll come to a junction. One of the nice features of this trail is that all the junctions are marked with a map on a signboard. Turn right at this junction, then left at the next. Already the trappings of urban life are beginning to recede. You'll soon be surrounded by oak and fir, trillium and ferns. If you're lucky, you might stumble across a black-tailed deer.

At the next junction, take a sharp right onto the Summit Trail. Despite the name of this trail and its obvious elevation, there aren't that many clear vistas from here; most are blocked by trees. But stay tuned; views are on the agenda for the second half of this walk. Keep climbing until you meet the West Ridge Trail, where you go left. Take the next two lefts as you loop around to return to the Summit Trail, heading north once again. This will take you back to your starting point, having completed the lower loop of the figure eight. For a bigger loop, you could opt to take the Park Loop Trail rather than the West Ridge Trail and still end up in the same place.

Once you've retraced your steps back to the trailhead at Southeast Sunnyside Road, cross the road and continue north onto Southeast 117th Avenue. Follow it north through quiet residential areas as it becomes first Southeast Southern Lites Drive (passing pleasant Southern Lites Park, which has access to its own network of trails and pretty Mount Scott Creek) and then veers right onto Southeast 119th Avenue. When you bump into Southeast William Otty Road, take a right. Then veer left onto Southeast 118th Court to find the trailhead at the entrance of ❷ **Mount Scott Nature Park.** Follow the footpath roughly northeast through the park to another trailhead at Southeast Greiner Lane. From here, turn sharply left as the trail meanders southwest back

Bonus Walk: Warrior Rock Lighthouse, Sauvie Island

Strictly speaking, this one is a little too far out of the way to qualify as a Portland walk, but Sauvie Island is so scenic and pleasant that we decided to throw in a walk here. Called Wappatoe Island by Lewis and Clark, Sauvie is a favorite getaway for Portlanders looking to pick fresh berries or see what that legendary nude beach is all about. It's a long, skinny island—about 15 miles by 4 miles—and about half of it is a designated wildlife area. Less than 500 people live on the island, although it used to be home to about a dozen Native American villages. It's about a 30-minute drive from Portland.

This 7-mile round-trip walk takes you to and from Warrior Rock, Oregon's smallest lighthouse. One of the few still-operational lighthouses *not* at the coast, it guides river traffic navigating the Columbia. A lighthouse has stood here since the 1880s. Once upon a time, lighthouse keepers had to use either a boat or an aerial cable (!) to reach it in high water, but operations are now automated.

The walk starts from the Warrior Rock trailhead at the end of Northwest Reeder Road. To get here, take US 30 toward St. Helens; in 8.5 miles you'll come to a stoplight, where you follow signs to turn right and cross the bridge connecting Sauvie Island to the mainland. Head north about 2 miles, then turn right onto Northwest Reeder Road. After about 10 miles, the road turns to gravel; drive 2.3 more miles to the trailhead parking lot.

The trail is a well-established out-and-back along the beach. It can get muddy in wet weather, so choose your footwear carefully. Parking permits ($10/day) are required; purchase at most general stores on the island.

through the park. As you head back from the Greiner Lane trailhead, look for a pair of decomposing old cars in the creekside gully that are slowly being swallowed up by the forest.

Backtrack slightly from this creek to the relatively new Studebaker Trail, where you start climbing uphill with the help of some steps made from massive logs. Mount Scott, at 1,090 feet, is the highest point in Southeast Portland, and you might feel the elevation gain on this walk. As you make your way west, consider venturing off-loop just a smidge to the alternative trailhead at Soloman Court for a great view of Mount Hood. In fact, part of the appeal of this route is that it gives you a completely different angle on your postcard snapshots of the city with the mountain on the horizon.

Wind your way west onto Southeast Hilltop Court until, just past Southeast Wahkeena Court, you come to ❸ The Stairs, which from here looks like a simple narrow sidewalk leading to the left. This winding path includes more than 400 stairs; apologies to your knees. When the stairs spit you out at Southeast William Otty Road, turn left and follow the road to complete the top half of the figure eight. This stretch also has plenty of views of Mount Talbert and Mount Hood.

Turn right (south) when you reach Southeast 119th Avenue, and retrace your steps to return to the bus stop on Southeast Sunnyside Road and the start of the walk.

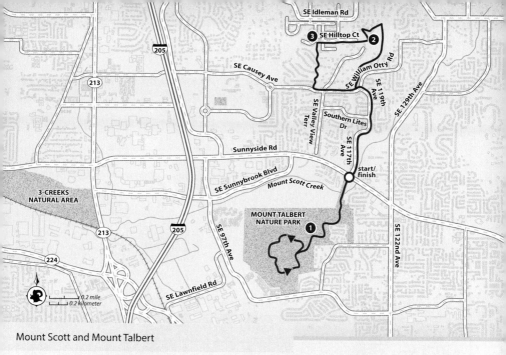

Mount Scott and Mount Talbert

Points of Interest

1 Mount Talbert Nature Park oregonmetro.gov/parks/mount-talbert-nature-park; 10945 SE Mather Road, Clackamas; 503-665-4995

2 Mount Scott Nature Park happyvalleyor.gov/community/parks-trails; 15410 SE Oregon Trail Dr., Happy Valley; 503-783-3800

3 The Stairs SE Hilltop Ct., Happy Valley

The Portland Aerial Tram (see Walk 11: Tram to South Waterfront, page 54)

Appendix: Walks by Theme

Park Life (*routes that include parks or forests*)
Downtown Park Blocks (Walk 2)
Goose Hollow (Walk 5)
Washington Park (Walk 6)
Forest Park (Walk 7)
Chapman School to Leif Erikson Drive (Walk 8)
Hawthorne Bridge to Steel Bridge (Walk 10)
Hawthorne Boulevard (Walk 14)
Stark-Belmont (Walk 15)
Kerns and Laurelhurst Park (Walk 17)
Fremont to Williams (Walk 21)
Historic Kenton (Walk 24)
St. Johns and Cathedral Park (Walk 25)
Columbia River Walk (Walk 26)
Lents (Walk 27)
Sellwood (Walk 29)
Fernhill Park to Woodlawn (Walk 31)
Milwaukie (Walk 32)

Eating and Drinking
Old Town and Chinatown (Walk 1)
Pearl District (Walk 3)
Northwest 21st and 23rd Avenues (Walk 4)
Industrial Southeast (Walk 12)
Division/Clinton, Ladd's Addition (Walk 13)
Hawthorne Boulevard (Walk 14)
Stark-Belmont (Walk 15)
Montavilla (Walk 16)
Kerns and Laurelhurst Park (Walk 17)
Irvington (Walk 18)
Hollywood (Walk 19)
Upper Sandy (Walk 20)
Fremont to Williams (Walk 21)
Mississippi to Killingsworth (Walk 22)
Alberta Arts District (Walk 23)
Multnomah Village (Walk 30)
Fernhill Park to Woodlawn (Walk 31)
Mount Scott and Mount Tabor (Walk 33)

History

Old Town and Chinatown (Walk 1)
Downtown Park Blocks (Walk 2)
Forest Park (Walk 7)
Reed College and Woodstock (Walk 28)

Up-and-Coming (*neighborhoods in flux*)

Nicolai and Slabtown (Walk 9)
Tram to South Waterfront (Walk 11)
Industrial Southeast (Walk 12)
Montavilla (Walk 16)
Fremont to Williams (Walk 21)
Milwaukie (Walk 32)

Rivers and Bridges

Old Town and Chinatown (Walk 1)
Hawthorne Bridge to Steel Bridge (Walk 10)
Tram to South Waterfront (Walk 11)
Hawthorne Boulevard (Walk 14)
St. Johns and Cathedral Park (Walk 25)
Columbia River Walk (Walk 26)
Sellwood (Walk 29)
Milwaukie (Walk 32)

Farther Afield (*walks that are slightly out of the way*)

Historic Kenton (Walk 24)
St. Johns and Cathedral Park (Walk 25)
Columbia River Walk (Walk 26)
Lents (Walk 27)
Multnomah Village (Walk 30)
Mount Scott and Mount Tabor (Walk 33)

Index

About the Author

Becky Ohlsen has lived in Portland since 1995. She is a freelance writer and editor who has contributed to a variety of publications, including the Pulitzer Prize–winning newsweekly *Willamette Week, The Oregonian, Portland Monthly,* and Lonely Planet, for which she has written several guidebooks about Scandinavia and the Pacific Northwest. She is also the author of new editions of *Backpacking Oregon, Best Tent Camping: Oregon,* and *One Night Wilderness: Portland,* all published by AdventureKEEN.